VGM Professional Resumes Series

SECOND EDITION

RESUMES FOR

ENVIRONMENTAL CAREERS

With Sample Cover Letters

The Editors of VGM Career Books

VGM Career Books

*Chicago   New York   San Francisco   Lisbon   London   Madrid   Mexico City
Milan   New Delhi   San Juan   Seoul   Singapore   Sydney   Toronto*

Library of Congress Cataloging-in-Publication Data

Resumes for environmental careers / the editors of VGM Career Book. — 2nd ed.
        p.   cm. — (VGM professional resumes series)
    ISBN 0-07-139042-1
    1. Environmental sciences—Vocational guidance.   2. Resumes (Employment)
3. Environmental protection—Vocational guidance.   4. Pollution control industry—
Vocational guidance.   I. VGM Career Books (Firm)   II. Series.
GE60 .R48   2002
    808'.06665—dc21   2002016856

1 2 3 4 5 6 7 8 9 0   QPD/QPD   1 0 9 8 7 6 5 4 3 2

ISBN 0-07-139042-1

McGraw-Hill books are available at special quantity discounts to use as premiums and
sales promotions, or for use in corporate training programs. For more information, please
write to the Director of Special Sales, Professional Publishing, McGraw-Hill, Two Penn
Plaza, New York, NY 10121-2298. Or contact your local bookstore.

This book is printed on acid-free paper.

Contents

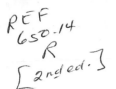

Introduction

Your resume is a piece of paper (or an electronic document) that serves to introduce you to the people who will eventually hire you. To write a thoughtful resume, you must thoroughly assess your personality, your accomplishments, and the skills you have acquired. The act of composing and submitting a resume also requires you to carefully consider the company or individual that might hire you. What are they looking for, and how can you meet their needs? This book shows you how to organize your personal information and experience into a concise and well-written resume, so that your qualifications and potential as an employee will be understood easily and quickly by a complete stranger.

Writing the resume is just one step in what can be a daunting job-search process, but it is an important element in the chain of events that will lead you to your new position. While you are probably a talented, bright, and charming person, your resume may not reflect these qualities. A poorly written resume can get you nowhere; a well-written resume can land you an interview and potentially a job. A good resume can even lead the interviewer to ask you questions that will allow you to talk about your strengths and highlight the skills you can bring to a prospective employer. Even a person with very little experience can find a good job if he or she is assisted by a thoughtful and polished resume.

Lengthy, typewritten resumes are a thing of the past. Today, employers do not have the time or the patience for verbose documents; they look for tightly composed, straightforward, action-based resumes. Although a one-page resume is the norm, a two-page resume may be warranted if you have had extensive job experience or have changed careers and truly need the space to properly position yourself. If, after careful editing, you still need more than one page to present yourself, it's acceptable to use a second page. A crowded resume that's hard to read would be the worst of your choices.

Distilling your work experience, education, and interests into such a small space requires preparation and thought. This book takes you step-by-step through the process of crafting an effective resume that will stand out in today's competitive marketplace. It serves as a workbook and a place to write down your experiences, while also including the techniques you'll need to pull all the necessary elements together. In the following pages, you'll find many examples of resumes that are specific to your area of interest. Study them for inspiration and find what appeals to you. There are a variety of ways to organize and present your information; inside, you'll find several that will be suitable to your needs. Good luck landing the job of your dreams!

The Elements of an Effective Resume

An effective resume is composed of information that employers are most interested in knowing about a prospective job applicant. This information is conveyed by a few essential elements. The following is a list of elements that are found in most resumes—some essential, some optional. Later in this chapter, we will further examine the role of each of these elements in the makeup of your resume.

- Heading

- Objective and/or Keyword Section

- Work Experience

- Education

- Honors

- Activities

- Certificates and Licenses

- Publications

- Professional Memberships

- Special Skills

- Personal Information

- References

The first step in preparing your resume is to gather information about yourself and your past accomplishments. Later you will refine this information, rewrite it using effective language, and organize it into an attractive layout. But first, let's take a look at each of these important elements individually so you can judge their appropriateness for your resume.

Heading

Although the heading may seem to be the simplest section of your resume, be careful not to take it lightly. It is the first section your prospective employer will see and it contains the information she or he will need to contact you. At the very least, the heading must contain your name, your home address, and, of course, a phone number where you can be reached easily.

In today's high-tech world, many of us have multiple ways that we can be contacted. You may list your E-mail address if you are reasonably sure the employer makes use of this form of communication. Keep in mind, however, that others may have access to your E-mail messages if you send them from an account provided by your current company. If this is a concern, do not list your work E-mail address on your resume. If you are able to take calls at your current place of business, you should include your work number, because most employers will attempt to contact you during typical business hours.

If you have voice mail or a reliable answering machine at home or at work, list its number in the heading and make sure your greeting is professional and clear. Always include at least one phone number in your heading, even if it is a temporary number, where a prospective employer can leave a message.

You might have a dozen different ways to be contacted, but you do not need to list all of them. Confine your numbers or addresses to those that are the easiest for the prospective employer to use and the simplest for you to retrieve.

Objective

When seeking a specific career path, it is important to list a job or career objective on your resume. This statement helps employers know the direction you see yourself taking, so they can determine whether your goals are in line with those of their organization and the position available. Normally, an objective is one to two sentences long. Its contents will vary depending on your career field, goals, and personality. The objective can be specific or general, but it should always be to the point. See the sample resumes in this book for examples.

If you are planning to use this resume online, or you suspect your potential employer is likely to scan your resume, you will want to include a "keyword" in the objective. This allows a prospective employer, searching hundreds of resumes for a specific skill or position objective, to locate the keyword and find your resume. In essence, a keyword is what's "hot" in your particular field at a given time. It's a buzzword, a shorthand way of getting a particular message across at a glance. For example, if you are a lawyer, your objective might state your desire to work in the area of corporate litigation. In this case, someone searching for the keyword "corporate litigation" will pull up your resume and know that you want to plan, research, and present cases at trial on behalf of the corporation. If your objective states that you "desire a challenging position in systems design," the keyword is "systems design," an industry-specific, shorthand way of saying that you want to be involved in assessing the need for, acquiring, and implementing high-technology systems. These are keywords and every industry has them, so it's becoming more and more important to include a few in your resume. (You may need to conduct additional research to make sure you know what keywords are most likely to be used in your desired industry, profession, or situation.)

There are many resume and job-search sites online. Like most things in the online world, they vary a great deal in quality. Use your discretion. If you plan to apply for jobs online or advertise your availability this way, you will want to design a scannable resume. This type of resume uses a format that can be easily scanned into a computer and added to a database. Scanning allows a prospective employer to use keywords to quickly review each applicant's experience and skills, and (in the event that there are many candidates for the job) to keep your resume for future reference.

Many people find that it is worthwhile to create two or more versions of their basic resume. You may want an intricately designed resume on high-quality paper to mail or hand out *and* a resume that is designed to be scanned into a computer and saved on a database or an online job site. You can even create a resume in ASCII text to E-mail to prospective employers. For further information, you may wish to refer to the *Guide to Internet Job Searching*, by Frances Roehm and Margaret Dikel, updated and published every other year by VGM Career Books, a division of the McGraw-Hill Companies. This excellent book contains helpful and detailed information about formatting a resume for Internet use. To get you started, in Chapter 3 we have included a list of things to keep in mind when creating electronic resumes.

Although it is usually a good idea to include an objective, in some cases this element is not necessary. The goal of the objective statement is to provide the employer with an idea of where you see yourself going in the field. However, if you are uncertain of the exact nature of the job you seek, including an objective that is too specific, could result in your not being considered for a host of perfectly acceptable positions. If you decide not to use an objective heading in your resume, you should definitely incorporate the information that would be conveyed in the objective into your cover letter.

Work Experience

Work experience is arguably the most important element of them all. Unless you are a recent graduate with little or no relevant work experience, your current and former positions will provide the central focus of the resume. You will want this section to be as complete and carefully constructed as possible. By thoroughly examining your work experience, you can get to the heart of your accomplishments and present them in a way that demonstrates and highlights your qualifications.

If you are just out of school, your resume will probably focus on your education, but you should also include information on your work or volunteer experiences. Although you will have less information about work experience than a person who has held multiple positions or is advanced in his or her career, the amount of information is not what is most important in this section. How the information is presented and what it says about you as a worker and a person is what really counts.

As you create this section of your resume, remember the need for accuracy. Include all the necessary information about each of your jobs, including your job title, dates of employment, name of your employer, city, state, responsibilities, special projects you handled, and accomplishments. Be sure to list only accomplishments for which you were directly responsible. And don't be alarmed if you haven't participated in or worked on special projects, because this section may not be relevant to certain jobs.

The most common way to list your work experience is in *reverse chronological order*. In other words, start with your most recent job and work your way backward. This way, your prospective employer sees your current (and often most important) position before considering your past employment. Your most recent position, if it's the most important in terms of responsibilities and relevance to the job for which you are applying, should also be the one that includes the most information as compared to your previous positions.

If you are just out of school, highlight your summer employment, internships, and part-time work. As a recent graduate, however, you will probably begin your resume with your education section. The experience you gain with "starter jobs" in the workplace and your ability to juggle school and employment are important to most employers, even if the work itself seems unrelated to your proposed career path. If you were promoted or given greater responsibilities or commendations, be sure to mention the fact.

The following worksheet is provided to help you organize your experiences in the working world. It will also serve as an excellent resource to refer to when updating your resume in the future.

WORK EXPERIENCE

Job One:

Job Title _____

Dates _____

Employer _____

City, State _____

Major Duties _____

_____

_____

_____

_____

_____

_____

_____

_____

Special Projects _____

_____

_____

_____

Accomplishments _____

_____

_____

_____

_____

_____

Job Two:

Job Title _____

Dates _____

Employer _____

City, State _____

Major Duties _____

_____

_____

_____

_____

_____

_____

_____

_____

Special Projects _____

_____

_____

_____

Accomplishments _____

_____

_____

_____

_____

_____

_____

_____

_____

Job Three:

Job Title _____

Dates _____

Employer _____

City, State _____

Major Duties _____

_____

_____

_____

_____

_____

_____

_____

Special Projects _____

_____

_____

_____

Accomplishments _____

_____

_____

_____

_____

_____

_____

_____

_____

Job Four:

Job Title _____

Dates _____

Employer _____

City, State _____

Major Duties _____

_____

_____

_____

_____

_____

_____

_____

_____

Special Projects _____

_____

_____

_____

Accomplishments _____

_____

_____

_____

_____

_____

_____

_____

_____

Education

Education is usually the second most important element of a resume. Your educational background is often a deciding factor in an employer's decision to interview you. Highlight your accomplishments in school as much as you did those accomplishments at work. If you are looking for your first professional job, your education will be your greatest asset because your related work experience will probably be minimal. In this case, the education section becomes the most important means of selling yourself.

Include in this section all the degrees or certificates you have received; your major or area of concentration; all of the honors you earned; and any relevant activities you participated in, organized, or chaired. Again, list your most recent schooling first. If you have completed graduate-level work, begin with that and work your way back through your undergraduate education. If you have completed college, you generally should not list your high school experience; do so only if you earned special honors, you had a grade point average that was much better than the norm, or this was your highest level of education.

If you have completed a large number of credit hours in a subject that may be relevant to the position you are seeking, but did not obtain a degree, you may wish to list the hours or classes you completed. Keep in mind, however, that you may be asked to explain why you did not finish the program. If you are currently in school, list the degree, certificate, or license you expect to obtain and the projected date of completion.

The following worksheet will help you gather the information you need for this section of your resume.

EDUCATION

School One _____

Major or Area of Concentration _____

Degree _____

Dates _____

School Two _____

Major or Area of Concentration _____

Degree _____

Dates _____

Honors

If you include an honors section in your resume, you should highlight any awards, honors, or memberships in honorary societies that you have received. (You may also incorporate this information into your education section.) Often, the honors are academic in nature, but this section also may be used for special achievements in sports, clubs, or other school activities. Always include the name of the organization awarding the honor and the date(s) received. Use the following worksheet to help you gather your information.

HONORS

Honor One _____

Awarding Organization _____

Date(s) _____

Honor Two _____

Awarding Organization _____

Date(s) _____

Honor Three _____

Awarding Organization _____

Date(s) _____

Honor Four _____

Awarding Organization _____

Date(s) _____

Honor Five _____

Awarding Organization _____

Date(s) _____

Activities

Perhaps you were active in different organizations or clubs during your years at school; often an employer will look at such involvement as evidence of initiative, dedication, and good social skills. Examples of your ability to take a leading role in a group should be included on a resume, if you can provide them. (Information about your activities also may be incorporated into your education section.) If you have been out of school for some time, the activities section of your resume can present neighborhood and community activities, volunteer positions, and so forth. In general, you may want to avoid listing any organization whose name indicates the race, creed, sex, age, marital status, sexual orientation, or nation of origin of its members because this could expose you to discrimination. Use the following worksheet to list the specifics of your activities.

ACTIVITIES

Organization/Activity _____

Accomplishments _____

_____

_____

Organization/Activity _____

Accomplishments _____

_____

_____

Organization/Activity _____

Accomplishments _____

_____

_____

As your work experience grows through the years, your school activities and honors will carry less weight and be emphasized less in your resume. Eventually, you will probably list only your degree and any major honors received. As time goes by, your job performance and the experience you've gained become the most important elements in your resume, which should change to reflect this.

Certificates and Licenses

If your chosen career path requires specialized training, you may already have certificates or licenses. You should list these if the job you are seeking requires them and you, of course, have acquired them. If you have applied for a license but have not yet received it, use the phrase "application pending."

License requirements vary by state. If you have moved or are planning to relocate to another state, check with that state's board or licensing agency for all licensing requirements.

Always make sure that all of the information you list is completely accurate. Locate copies of your certificates and licenses, and check the exact date and name of the accrediting agency. Use the following worksheet to organize the necessary information.

CERTIFICATES AND LICENSES

Name of License _____

Licensing Agency _____

Date Issued _____

Name of License _____

Licensing Agency _____

Date Issued _____

Name of License _____

Licensing Agency _____

Date Issued _____

Publications

Some professions strongly encourage or even require that you publish. If you have written, coauthored, or edited any books, articles, professional papers, or works of a similar nature that pertain to your field, you will definitely want to include this element. Remember to list the date of publication and the publisher's name, and specify whether you were the sole author or a coauthor. Book, magazine, or journal titles are generally italicized, while the titles of articles within a larger publication appear in quotes. (Check with your reference librarian for more about the appropriate way to present this information.) For scientific or research papers, you will need to give the date, place, and audience to whom the paper was presented.

Use the following worksheet to help you gather the necessary information about your publications.

PUBLICATIONS

Title and Type (Note, Article, etc.) _____

Title of Publication (Journal, Book, etc.) _____

Publisher _____

Date Published _____

Title and Type (Note, Article, etc.) _____

Title of Publication (Journal, Book, etc.) _____

Publisher _____

Date Published _____

Title and Type (Note, Article, etc.) _____

Title of Publication (Journal, Book, etc.) _____

Publisher _____

Date Published _____

Professional Memberships

Another potential element in your resume is a section listing professional memberships. Use this section to describe your involvement in professional associations, unions, and similar organizations. It is to your advantage to list any professional memberships that pertain to the job you are seeking. Many employers see your membership as representative of your desire to stay up-to-date and connected in your field. Include the dates of your involvement and whether you took part in any special activities or held any offices within the organization. Use the following worksheet to organize your information.

PROFESSIONAL MEMBERSHIPS

Name of Organization _____

Office(s) Held_____

Activities _____

Dates _____

Name of Organization _____

Office(s) Held_____

Activities _____

Dates _____

Name of Organization _____

Office(s) Held_____

Activities _____

Dates _____

Name of Organization _____

Office(s) Held_____

Activities _____

Dates _____

Special Skills

The special skills section of your resume is the place to mention any special abilities you have that relate to the job you are seeking. You can use this element to present certain talents or experiences that are not necessarily a part of your education or work experience. Common examples include fluency in a foreign language, extensive travel abroad, or knowledge of a particular computer application. "Special skills" can encompass a wide range of talents, and this section can be used creatively. However, for each skill you list, you should be able to describe how it would be a direct asset in the type of work you're seeking because employers may ask just that in an interview. If you can't think of a way to do this, it may be extraneous information.

Personal Information

Some people include personal information on their resumes. This is generally not recommended, but you might wish to include it if you think that something in your personal life, such as a hobby or talent, has some bearing on the position you are seeking. This type of information is often referred to at the beginning of an interview, when it may be used as an "icebreaker." Of course, personal information regarding your age, marital status, race, religion, or sexual orientation should never appear on your resume as *personal information*. It should be given only in the context of memberships and activities, and only when doing so would not expose you to discrimination.

References

References are not usually given on the resume itself, but a prospective employer needs to know that you have references who may be contacted if necessary. All you need to include is a single sentence at the end of the resume: "References are available upon request," or even simply, "References available." Have a reference list ready—your interviewer may ask to see it! Contact each person on the list ahead of time to see whether it is all right for you to use him or her as a reference. This way, the person has a chance to think about what to say *before* the call occurs. This helps ensure that you will obtain the best reference possible.

Writing Your Resume

Now that you have gathered the information for each section of your resume, it's time to write it out in a way that will get the attention of the reviewer—hopefully, your future employer! The language you use in your resume will affect its success, so you must be careful and conscientious. Translate the facts you have gathered into the active, precise language of resume writing. You will be aiming for a resume that keeps the reader's interest and highlights your accomplishments in a concise and effective way.

Resume writing is unlike any other form of writing. Although your seventh-grade composition teacher would not approve, the rules of punctuation and sentence building are often completely ignored. Instead, you should try for a functional, direct writing style that focuses on the use of verbs and other words that imply action on your part. Writing with action words and strong verbs characterizes you to potential employers as an energetic, active person, someone who completes tasks and achieves results from his or her work. Resumes that do not make use of action words can sound passive and stale. These resumes are not effective and do not get the attention of any employer, no matter how qualified the applicant. Choose words that display your strengths and demonstrate your initiative. The following list of commonly used verbs will help you create a strong resume:

administered	assembled
advised	assumed responsibility
analyzed	billed
arranged	built

carried out	inspected
channeled	interviewed
collected	introduced
communicated	invented
compiled	maintained
completed	managed
conducted	met with
contacted	motivated
contracted	negotiated
coordinated	operated
counseled	orchestrated
created	ordered
cut	organized
designed	oversaw
determined	performed
developed	planned
directed	prepared
dispatched	presented
distributed	produced
documented	programmed
edited	published
established	purchased
expanded	recommended
functioned as	recorded
gathered	reduced
handled	referred
hired	represented
implemented	researched
improved	reviewed

saved	supervised
screened	taught
served as	tested
served on	trained
sold	typed
suggested	wrote

Let's look at two examples that differ only in their writing style. The first resume section is ineffective because it does not use action words to accent the applicant's work experiences:

WORK EXPERIENCE
Regional Sales Manager

Manager of sales representatives from seven states. Manager of twelve food chain accounts in the East. In charge of the sales force's planned selling toward specific goals. Supervisor and trainer of new sales representatives. Consulting for customers in the areas of inventory management and quality control.

Special Projects: Coordinator and sponsor of annual food industry sales seminar.

Accomplishments: Monthly regional volume went up 25 percent during my tenure while, at the same time, a proper sales/cost ratio was maintained. Customer-company relations were improved.

In the following paragraph, we have rewritten the same section using action words. Notice how the tone has changed. It now sounds stronger and more active. This person accomplished goals and really *did* things.

WORK EXPERIENCE
Regional Sales Manager

Managed sales representatives from seven states. Oversaw twelve food chain accounts in the eastern United States. Directed the sales force in planned selling toward specific goals. Supervised and trained new sales representatives. Counseled customers in the areas of inventory management and quality control. Coordinated and sponsored the annual Food Industry Seminar. Increased monthly regional volume 25 percent and helped to improve customer-company relations during my tenure.

One helpful way to construct the work experience section is to make use of your actual job descriptions—the written duties and expectations your employers had for a person in your current or former position. Job descriptions are rarely written in proper resume language, so you will have to rework them, but they do include much of the information necessary to create this section of your resume. If you have access to job descriptions for your former positions, you can use the details to construct an action-oriented paragraph. Often, your human resources department can provide a job description for your current position.

The following is an example of a typical human resources job description, followed by a rewritten version of the same description employing action words and specific details about the job. Again, pay attention to the style of writing instead of the content, as the details of your own experience will be unique.

WORK EXPERIENCE
Public Administrator I

Responsibilities: Coordinate and direct public services to meet the needs of the nation, state, or community. Analyze problems; work with special committees and public agencies; recommend solutions to governing bodies.

Aptitudes and Skills: Ability to relate to and communicate with people; solve complex problems through analysis; plan, organize, and implement policies and programs. Knowledge of political systems, financial management, personnel administration, program evaluation, and organizational theory.

WORK EXPERIENCE
Public Administrator I

Wrote pamphlets and conducted discussion groups to inform citizens of legislative processes and consumer issues. Organized and supervised 25 interviewers. Trained interviewers in effective communication skills.

After you have written out your resume, you are ready to begin the next important step: assembly and layout.

Chapter 3

Assembly and Layout

At this point, you've gathered all the necessary information for your resume and rewritten it in language that will impress your potential employers. Your next step is to assemble the sections in a logical order and lay them out on the page neatly and attractively to achieve the desired effect: getting the interview.

Assembly

The order of the elements in a resume makes a difference in its overall effect. Clearly, you would not want to bury your name and address somewhere in the middle of the resume. Nor would you want to lead with a less important section, such as special skills. Put the elements in an order that stresses your most important accomplishments and the things that will be most appealing to your potential employer. For example, if you recently graduated from school and have no full-time work experience, you will want the reviewer to read about your education before any part-time jobs you may have held during the vacations. On the other hand, if you have been gainfully employed for several years and currently hold an important position in your company, you should list your work accomplishments ahead of your educational information, which has become less pertinent with time.

Certain things should always be included in your resume, but others are optional. The following list shows you which are which. You might want to use it as a checklist to be certain that you have included all of the necessary information.

Essential	**Optional**
Name	Cellular Phone Number
Address	Pager Number
Phone Number	E-Mail Address or Website Address
Work Experience	Voice Mail Number
Education	Job Objective
References Phrase	Honors
	Special Skills
	Publications
	Professional Memberships
	Activities
	Certificates and Licenses
	Personal Information
	Graphics
	Photograph

Your choice of optional sections depends on your own background and employment needs. Always use information that will put you in a favorable light—unless it's absolutely essential, avoid anything that will prompt the interviewer to ask questions about your weaknesses or something else that could be unflattering. Make sure your information is accurate and truthful. If your honors are impressive, include them in the resume. If your activities in school demonstrate talents that are necessary for the job you are seeking, allow space for a section on activities. If you are applying for a position that requires ornamental illustration, you may want to include border illustrations or graphics that demonstrate your talents in this area. If you are answering an advertisement for a job that requires certain physical traits, a photo of yourself might be appropriate. A person applying for a job as a computer programmer would *not* include a photo as part of his or her resume. Each resume is unique, just as each person is unique.

Types of Resumes

So far we have focused on the most common type of resume—the *reverse chronological* resume—in which your most recent job is listed first. This is the type of resume usually preferred by those who have to read a large number of resumes, and it is by far the most popular and widely circulated. However, this style of presentation may not be the most effective way to highlight *your* skills and accomplishments.

For example, if you are reentering the workforce after many years or are trying to change career fields, the *functional* resume may work best. This type of resume puts the focus on your achievements instead of the sequence of your work history. In the functional resume, your experience is presented through your general accomplishments and the skills you have developed in your working life.

A functional resume is assembled from the same information you gathered in Chapter 1. The main difference lies in how you organize the information. Essentially, the work experience section is divided in two, with your job duties and accomplishments constituting one section and your employers' names, cities, and states; your positions; and the dates employed making up the other. Place the first section near the top of your resume, just below your job objective (if used), and call it *Accomplishments* or *Achievements*. The second section, containing the bare essentials of your work history, should come after the accomplishments section and can be called *Employment History*, since it is a chronological overview of your former jobs.

The other sections of your resume remain the same. The work experience section is the only one affected in the functional format. By placing the section that focuses on your achievements at the beginning, you draw attention to these achievements. This puts less emphasis on whom you worked for and when, and more on what you did and what you are capable of doing.

If you are changing careers, the emphasis on skills and achievements is important. The identities of previous employers (who aren't part of your new career field) need to be downplayed. A functional resume can help accomplish this task. If you are reentering the workforce after a long absence, a functional resume is the obvious choice. And if you lack full-time work experience, you will need to draw attention away from this fact and put the focus on your skills and abilities. You may need to highlight your volunteer activities and part-time work. Education may also play a more important role in your resume.

The type of resume that is right for you will depend on your personal circumstances. It may be helpful to create both types and then compare them. Which one presents you in the best light? Examples of both types of resumes are included in this book. Use the sample resumes in Chapter 5 to help you decide on the content, presentation, and look of your own resume.

Special Tips for Electronic Resumes

Because there are many details to consider in writing a resume that will be posted or transmitted on the Internet, or one that will be scanned into a computer when it is received, we suggest that you refer to the *Guide to Internet Job Searching*, by Frances Roehm and Margaret Dikel, as previously mentioned. However, here are some brief, general guidelines to follow if you expect your resume to be scanned into a computer.

- Use standard fonts in which none of the letters touch.

- Keep in mind that underlining, italics, and fancy scripts may not scan well.

- Use boldface and capitalization to set off elements. Again, make sure letters don't touch. Leave at least a quarter inch between lines of type.

- Keep information and elements at the left margin. Centering, columns, and even indenting may change when the resume is optically scanned.

- Do not use any lines, boxes, or graphics.

- Place the most important information at the top of the first page. If you use two pages, put "Page 1 of 2" at the bottom of the first page and put your name and "Page 2 of 2" at the top of the second page.

- List each telephone number on its own line in the header.

- Use multiple keywords or synonyms for what you do to make sure your qualifications will be picked up if a prospective employer is searching for them. Use nouns that are keywords for your profession.

- Be descriptive in your titles. For example, don't just use "assistant"; use "legal office assistant."

- Make sure the contrast between print and paper is good. Use a high-quality laser printer and white or very light-colored 8½-by-11-inch paper.

- Mail a high-quality laser print or an excellent copy. Do not fold or use staples, as this might interfere with scanning. You may, however, use paper clips.

In addition to creating a resume that works well for scanning, you may want to have a resume that can be E-mailed to reviewers. Because you may not know what word processing application the recipient uses, the best format to use is ASCII text. (ASCII stands for "American Standard Code for Information Exchange.") It allows people with very different software platforms to exchange and understand information. (E-mail operates on this principle.) ASCII is a simple, text-only language, which means you can include only simple text. There can be no use of boldface, italics, or even paragraph indentations.

To create an ASCII resume, just use your normal word processing program; when finished, save it as a "text only" document. You will find this option under the "save" or "save as" command. Here is a list of things to *avoid* when crafting your electronic resume:

- Tabs. Use your space bar. Tabs will not work.

- Any special characters, such as mathematical symbols.

- Word wrap. Use hard returns (the return key) to make line breaks.

- Centering or other formatting. Align everything at the left margin.

- Bold or italic fonts. Everything will be converted to plain text when you save the file as a "text only" document.

Check carefully for any mistakes before you save the document as a text file. Spellcheck and proofread it several times, then ask someone with a keen eye to go over it again for you. Remember: the key is to keep it simple. Any attempt to make this resume pretty or decorative may result in a resume that is confusing and hard to read. After you have saved the document, you can cut and paste it into an E-mail or onto a website.

Layout for a Paper Resume

A great deal of care—and much more formatting—is necessary to achieve an attractive layout for your paper resume. There is no single appropriate layout that applies to every resume, but there are a few basic rules to follow in putting your resume on paper:

- Leave a comfortable margin on the sides, top, and bottom of the page (usually one to one and a half inches).

- Use appropriate spacing between the sections (two to three line spaces are usually adequate).

- Be consistent in the *type* of headings you use for different sections of your resume. For example, if you capitalize the heading EMPLOYMENT HISTORY, don't use initial capitals and underlining for a section of equal importance, such as <u>Education</u>.

- Do not use more than one font in your resume. Stay consistent by choosing a font that is fairly standard and easy to read, and don't change it for different sections. Beware of the tendency to try to make your resume original by choosing fancy type styles; your resume may end up looking unprofessional instead of creative. Unless you are in a very creative and artistic field, you should almost always stick with tried-and-true type styles like Times New Roman and Palatino, which are often used in business writing. In the area of resume styles, conservative is usually the best way to go.

- Always try to fit your resume on one page. If you are having trouble with this, you may be trying to say too much. Edit out any repetitive or unnecessary information, and shorten descriptions of earlier jobs where possible. Ask a friend you trust for feedback on what seems unnecessary or unimportant. For example, you may have included too many optional sections. Today, with the prevalence of the personal computer as a tool, there is no excuse for a poorly laid-out resume. Experiment with variations until you are pleased with the result.

CHRONOLOGICAL RESUME

Lucas Jackson
2399 S. Division • Grand Rapids, MI 49503
(616) 555-9354
Cell: (616) 555-2819
lucasjackson@xxx.com

Objective

Apply my skills as a content expert to a new challenge with a company focused on quality, dedication, and ingenuity.

Work

1998 to present

Content Strategist, Sonic Consulting, Grand Rapids, MI

> Provide digital solutions for clients interested in establishing their presence online. Make recommendations on content assets, third-party content partnerships, and content management systems. Direct copywriters and design teams to fulfill the clients' objectives and create brand strategies.

1996 to 1998

Website Manager, *Crash! Magazine*, Detroit, MI

> Directed the online version of *Crash! Magazine* and ensured design and content guidelines of the site followed those of the print version. Coordinated special events to drive traffic to the site resulting in a 75 percent increase in hits over four months. Created and edited content specifically for the site to establish its own identity.

1994 to 1996

Writer, *Digital City Magazine*, Detroit, MI

> Researched and wrote articles covering the emerging Internet business and issues that relate to that unique business sector. Interviewed people involved in cutting-edge development on the Web and analyzed the business implications of this unique medium.

Skills

- Intimate familiarity with standard style guides including *AP, Chicago Manual, MLA,* and *Wired.*
- Very knowledgeable in the use and merits of content management systems such as Vignette, ePrise, and BroadVision.
- Uncanny ability to merge creative vision with business objectives to create distinctive and engaging content.

References available upon request

FUNCTIONAL RESUME

Katrina Parker
1402 Greenbriar Road
Charleston, WV 25304
(304) 555-1704

Applications & Systems Programmer

Credentials

- B.S. in Computer Science—March 1995—University of Michigan; minor in Accounting
- Knowledge of COBOL, FORTRAN, Pascal, C, C Plus, BASIC, CAD/CAM, RPG II, ASSEMBLY language #68000, 8086 & 6502, and dbase
- High level of self-motivation and attention to detail

Job Duties

- Code, test, debug, and maintain programs
- Create program documentation
- Integrate new hardware into existing systems
- Diagnose and correct systems failures
- Maintain monitors, database packages, compilers, assemblers, and utility programs
- Select and modify new hardware and software to company specifications

Achievements

- Designed programs in C Plus for Heritage Bank to coordinate functions of ATM machines
- Purchased new hardware and software for Advantage Publishers, modified equipment to suit company's needs and resolve interoperability issues

Employers

Heritage Bank	6/99 to Present
Advantage Publishers	4/96 to 6/99

References

Marta Dalton	Renu Das
Vice President of Finance	Director of Human Resources
Heritage Bank	Advantage Publishers
411 Watkins Street	694 Dale Street
Charleston, WV 25304	Deer Park, NY 11729
(304) 555-2225, Ext. 203	(516) 555-7937

Remember that a resume is not an autobiography. Too much information will only get in the way. The more compact your resume, the easier it will be to review. If a person who is swamped with resumes looks at yours, catches the main points, and then calls you for an interview to fill in some of the details, your resume has already accomplished its task. A clear and concise resume makes for a happy reader and a good impression.

There are times when, despite extensive editing, the resume simply cannot fit on one page. In this case, the resume should be laid out on two pages in such a way that neither clarity nor appearance is compromised. Each page of a two-page resume should be marked clearly: the first should indicate "Page 1 of 2," and the second should include your name and the page number, for example, "Julia Ramirez—Page 2 of 2." The pages should then be stapled together. You may use a smaller font (in the same font as the body of your resume) for the page numbers. Place them at the bottom of page one and the top of page two. Again, spend the time now to experiment with the layout until you find one that looks good to you.

Always show your final layout to other people and ask them what they like or dislike about it, and what impresses them most when they read your resume. Make sure that their responses are the same as what you want to elicit from your prospective employer. If they aren't the same, you should continue to make changes until the necessary information is emphasized.

Proofreading

After you have finished typing the master copy of your resume and before you have it copied or printed, thoroughly check it for typing and spelling errors. Do not place all your trust in your computer's spellcheck function. Use an old editing trick and read the whole resume backward—start at the end and read it right to left and bottom to top. This can help you see the small errors or inconsistencies that are easy to overlook. Take time to do it right because a single error on a document this important can cause the reader to judge your attention to detail in a harsh light.

Have several people look at the finished resume just in case you've missed an error. Don't try to take a shortcut; not having an unbiased set of eyes examine your resume now could mean embarrassment later. Even experienced editors can easily overlook their own errors. Be thorough and conscientious with your proofreading so your first impression is a perfect one.

We have included the following rules of capitalization and punctuation to assist you in the final stage of creating your resume. Remember that resumes often require use of a shorthand style of writing that may include sentences without periods and other stylistic choices that break the standard rules of grammar. Be consistent in each section, and throughout the whole resume, with your choices.

RULES OF CAPITALIZATION

- Capitalize proper nouns, such as names of schools, colleges, and universities; names of companies; and brand names of products.

- Capitalize major words in the names and titles of books, tests, and articles that appear in the body of your resume.

- Capitalize words in major section headings of your resume.

- Do not capitalize words just because they seem important.

- When in doubt, consult a manual of style such as *Words into Type* (Prentice-Hall) or *The Chicago Manual of Style* (The University of Chicago Press). Your local library can help you locate these and other reference books. Many computer programs also have grammar help sections.

RULES OF PUNCTUATION

- Use commas to separate words in a series.

- Use a semicolon to separate series of words that already include commas within the series. (For an example, see the first rule of capitalization.)

- Use a semicolon to separate independent clauses that are not joined by a conjunction.

- Use a period to end a sentence.

- Use a colon to show that examples or details follow that will expand or amplify the preceding phrase.

- Avoid the use of dashes.

- Avoid the use of brackets.

- If you use any punctuation in an unusual way in your resume, be consistent in its use.

- Whenever you are uncertain, consult a style manual.

Putting Your Resume in Print

You will need to buy high-quality paper for your printer before you print your finished resume. Regular office paper is not good enough for resumes; the reviewer will probably think it looks flimsy and cheap. Go to an office supply store or copy shop and select a high-quality bond paper that will make a good first impression. Select colors like white, off-white, or possibly a light gray. In some industries, a pastel may be acceptable, but be sure the color and feel of the paper makes a subtle, positive statement about you. Nothing in the choice of paper should be loud or unprofessional.

If your computer printer does not reproduce your resume properly and produces smudged or stuttered type, either ask to borrow a friend's or take your disk (or a clean original) to a printer or copy shop for high-quality copying. If you anticipate needing a large number of copies, taking your resume to a copy shop or a printer is probably the best choice.

Hold a sheet of your unprinted bond paper up to the light. If it has a watermark, you will want to point this out to the person helping you with copies; the printing should be done so that the reader can read the print and see the watermark the right way up. Check each copy for smudges or streaks. This is the time to be a perfectionist—the results of your careful preparation will be well worth it.

The Cover Letter

Once your resume has been assembled, laid out, and printed to your satisfaction, the next and final step before distribution is to write your cover letter. Though there may be instances where you deliver your resume in person, you will usually send it through the mail or online. Resumes sent through the mail always need an accompanying letter that briefly introduces you and your resume. The purpose of the cover letter is to get a potential employer to read your resume, just as the purpose of the resume is to get that same potential employer to call you for an interview.

Like your resume, your cover letter should be clean, neat, and direct. A cover letter usually includes the following information:

1. Your name and address (unless it already appears on your personal letterhead) and your phone number(s); see item 7.

2. The date.

3. The name and address of the person and company to whom you are sending your resume.

4. The salutation ("Dear Mr." or "Dear Ms." followed by the person's last name, or "To Whom It May Concern" if you are answering a blind ad).

5. An opening paragraph explaining why you are writing (for example, in response to an ad, as a follow-up to a previous meeting, at the suggestion of someone you both know) and indicating that you are interested in whatever job is being offered.

6. One or more paragraphs that tell why you want to work for the company and what qualifications and experiences you can bring to the position. This is a good place to mention some detail about

that particular company that makes you want to work for them; this shows that you have done some research before applying.

7. A final paragraph that closes the letter and invites the reviewer to contact you for an interview. This can be a good place to tell the potential employer which method would be best to use when contacting you. Be sure to give the correct phone number and a good time to reach you, if that is important. You may mention here that your references are available upon request.

8. The closing ("Sincerely" or "Yours truly") followed by your signature in a dark ink, with your name typed under it.

Your cover letter should include all of this information and be no longer than one page in length. The language used should be polite, businesslike, and to the point. Don't attempt to tell your life story in the cover letter; a long and cluttered letter will serve only to annoy the reader. Remember that you need to mention only a few of your accomplishments and skills in the cover letter. The rest of your information is available in your resume. If your cover letter is a success, your resume will be read and all pertinent information reviewed by your prospective employer.

Producing the Cover Letter

Cover letters should always be individualized because they are always written to specific individuals and companies. Never use a form letter for your cover letter or copy it as you would a resume. Each cover letter should be unique, and as personal and lively as possible. (Of course, once you have written and rewritten your first cover letter until you are satisfied with it, you can certainly use similar wording in subsequent letters. You may want to save a template on your computer for future reference.) Keep a hard copy of each cover letter so you know exactly what you wrote in each one.

There are sample cover letters in Chapter 6. Use them as models or for ideas of how to assemble and lay out your own cover letters. Remember that every letter is unique and depends on the particular circumstances of the individual writing it and the job for which he or she is applying.

After you have written your cover letter, proofread it as thoroughly as you did your resume. Again, spelling or punctuation errors are a sure sign of carelessness, and you don't want that to be a part of your first impression on a prospective employer. This is no time to trust your spellcheck function. Even after going through a spelling and grammar check, your cover letter should be carefully proofread by at least one other person.

Print the cover letter on the same quality bond paper you used for your resume. Remember to sign it, using a good, dark-ink pen. Handle the letter and resume carefully to avoid smudging or wrinkling, and mail them together in an appropriately sized envelope. Many stores sell matching envelopes to coordinate with your choice of bond paper.

Keep an accurate record of all resumes you send out and the results of each mailing. This record can be kept on your computer, in a calendar or notebook, or on file cards. Knowing when a resume is likely to have been received will keep you on track as you make follow-up phone calls.

About a week after mailing resumes and cover letters to potential employers, contact them by telephone. Confirm that your resume arrived and ask whether an interview might be possible. Be sure to record the name of the person you spoke to and any other information you gleaned from the conversation. It is wise to treat the person answering the phone with a great deal of respect; sometimes the assistant or receptionist has the ear of the person doing the hiring.

You should make a great impression with the strong, straightforward resume and personalized cover letter you have just created. We wish you every success in securing the career of your dreams!

Sample Resumes

Thissample chapter contains dozens of sample resumes for people pursuing a wide variety of jobs and careers within this field.

There are many different styles of resumes in terms of graphic layout and presentation of information. These samples also represent people with varying amounts of education and work experience. Use these samples to model your own resume after. Choose one resume, or borrow elements from several different resumes to help you construct your own.

COREY W. V. MICHNER

22 NE 56th Street
Pittsburgh, PA 15244
412-555-3742

OBJECTIVE

A supervisory/management position with an environmental firm that will challenge and enhance my experience, knowledge, skills, and years of increasing responsibility.

HIGHLIGHTS OF QUALIFICATIONS

- Twenty-three years of experience in managing and supervising facilities, equipment, and personnel.
- Experience in toxic waste handling and related environmental protection issues.
- Supervision of over 100 personnel.
- Extensive skills in planning, coordinating, and supervising of projects.
- Reliable and adaptable; learn new systems quickly and take initiative.
- Professional appearance and manner.

WORK EXPERIENCE

Operation Supervisor, Suver Pennsylvania Compost Company, Inc. 1990–present.
- Control plant operations of 600 ton-per-day MSW facility with over 100 employees.
- Assume full responsibilities in absence of plant manager.
- Interview and hire employees, create work schedules, and perform daily production and technical inspections of equipment.
- Participate in daily performance testing.
- Train all personnel.

Superintendent, Suver Waste Systems, Kingley Fast Disposal. 1986–1990.
- Assumed responsibility for closure of KFD Landfill.
- Coordinated employee work schedules for 10 personnel, truck delivery of closure material, and work schedules of subcontractors tasked with installation of PVC liner.
- Solved soil erosion problems economically.
- Scheduled maintenance for and operated heavy equipment.
- Made purchases for daily operations.

page 1 of 2

Group Engineer, Commissioned Chief Warrant Officer, U.S. Coast Guard. 1982–1986.
- Directed all civil and naval engineering support.
- Supervised over 100 maintenance personnel for large patrol boats, small boats, and Coast Guard facilities, including various duty stations and 97 housing units.
- Oversaw personnel training budget management, and procurement for a department with a $250,000 annual budget and individual contracts in excess of $80,000.
- Served as Safety Officer, Hazardous Waste Officer, and Energy Conservation Coordinator.

Senior Chief Machinery Technician, U.S. Coast Guard. 1980–1982.
- Managed maintenance of two Coast Guard stations, two large patrol boats, and several small boats, including electrical, propulsion, and hydraulic systems.
- Developed computerized maintenance project list, administered budget, and supervised over 50 personnel.

EDUCATION
U.S. Coast Guard
Hazardous Waste Management, Leadership and Management, Procurement and Contraction, Oil Pollution and Law Enforcement, Collateral Duty Safety Officer, FBI Self-Defense and Arrest Procedures, Emergency Medical Technician, First Aid, and Personal Protection.

Western Missouri State College
General Studies. 1978–1980.

REFERENCES
Furnished immediately on request.

JACK COCHRAN

224 Foxpark Road   Laramie, WY 82057   (307) 555-8532

SUMMARY

Seeking environmental technology position with company actively involved in geological structures and analysis. Excellent skills in problem solving, analytical thinking, and client relations complement an engineering background. Self-sufficient, industrious, organized, and work well with others.

EDUCATION

B.S. in Geology, California State University, Chico, CA, 1993.
Pursued additional coursework in Engineering at California Polytechnic State University, San Luis Obispo, CA, 1990.

Geology Courses	Engineering Courses
Geologic Mapping	Engineering Materials
Geology Field Camp	Engineering Physics I, II, III
Structural Geology	Metallurgical Engineering I
Sedimentary Petrology	Thermodynamics I
Igneous Petrology	Chemistry I, II, III
Metamorphic Petrology	Calculus I, II, III
Geochemistry	Linear Algebra
Optical Crystallography	
X-Ray Crystallography	

EXPERIENCE

SNL Laboratories, Piedmont, TX, Core Analyst, 1999–2002.
Retrieved, catalogued, and preserved orientation of cores from oil fields and Superfund sites. Represented company in the field. Described lithologies on-site and in lab. Prepared samples of core by slabbing, photographing, selecting sample location, and plugging. Measured porosity, permeability, oil saturation, and gamma log response. Laid out core and discussed analysis with clients.

Buzz Newport Construction, Hayward, CA, Framing Foreman, 1993–1999.
Built, remodeled, and restored large, custom homes in old, exclusive neighborhood for contracting firm. Worked in all phases of construction. Prepared layout from architects' plans. Framed houses from foundation to roof. Supervised assistant carpenters and laborers. Coordinated subcontractors. Maintained client relationships and informed clients of progress.

REFERENCES

Available upon request.

JUDITH W. SWENSEN
4422 Kennet Avenue
Jubal, Tennessee 37232
615/555-4876

SUMMARY OF QUALIFICATIONS

Provide comprehensive environmental assistance to mining operations and exploration projects. Maintain awareness of all federal environmental regulations to assess compliance of subsidiary companies. Conduct detailed environment audits at mining and terminal locations.

ACCOMPLISHMENTS

Solid Waste Disposal

Determine best possible disposal method at each subsidiary mine. Choose site-specific methods depending on depth to groundwater ratio, percentage and types of heavy metals present in the coal ash, and column leachate test results of coal ash alone and coal ash mixed with coarse coal refuse. Investigate utilization of coal ash for construction of concrete block stoppings and timbers for roof control in underground mines. Investigated and designed economical solid and hazardous waste disposal options for subsidiary companies.

Mine Drainage Treatment

Develop methods to economically and effectively treat acid mine drainage (AMD) microbial troughs and anoxic drains with rapid progress toward successful conclusion and development. Assisted subsidiaries with effective, economical methods of controlling AMD from coal refuse piles to ensure reclamation success. Conducted research with Tennessee State University to determine methods of refuse pretreatment to eliminate future AMD and successfully installed two systems.

EMPLOYMENT HISTORY

Senior Environmental Specialist, 1992 to present
Smoky Mountain Mining Company, Memphis, Tennessee

Graduate Assistant/Lab Technician, 1989 to 1992
University of Tennessee, Chemical Engineering Department, Knoxville

EDUCATION

University of Tennessee
Ph.D., Chemical Engineering, 1992
B.S., Chemistry and Physics, 1989

REFERENCES

Available upon request

CHE V. JUAREZ
22 S. Gordon Ave.
Dallas, Texas 75232
214/555-4459

PROFESSIONAL OBJECTIVE
Seeking a management position with an environmental organization involved with developing and maintaining resources. Specifically interested in work requiring interaction with government agencies and legislative bodies.

MAJOR EMPLOYMENT EXPERIENCE AND ACCOMPLISHMENTS
June 1989 to present
ENVIRONMENTAL ADVOCATES -- Dallas, Texas
Legislative Liaison
Lobby, address, and monitor all proposed legislation for start-up seed money for small businesses as part of the state's environmental protection bill. Work closely with several organizations to promote the sensitive development of resources. Write action plans for 5- and 10-year energy and natural resource preservation.

March 1987 to November 1989
ITT COMMUNICATIONS -- Houston, Texas
District Manager
Managed nine counties for sales and service. Prepared a budget and sales forecast for the service shop and sales staff. Directed support and overhead costs, revenue projections, personnel management, sales and service programs, public relations, and mountaintop site development and management. Employed the pinpoint marketing technique I developed at CBG Electronics.

September 1982 to February 1987
CBG ELECTRONICS DIVISION -- Dallas, Texas
Service Manager/Marketing Manager
Managed servicing and maintenance, mountaintop site development, frequency coordination, customer relations for system changes, and marketing. Designed a pinpoint marketing approach to sales efforts based on a study of market trends and license application histories that proved extremely effective. Promoted this practice to the firm's sales and service personnel. Promoted radio/telephone systems to rural fire and police protection agencies. Assumed responsibility for developing several mountaintop communication sites, power transmission lines, tower design and construction, access roads, pipelines, and generator facilities.

EDUCATION
Southern Methodist University
Dallas, Texas
B.S. -- Communications

University of Washington
Seattle, Washington
Business Administration Studies

PROFESSIONAL ORGANIZATIONS
National Association of Environmental Professionals
Society for Technical Communication

EXTENDED EDUCATION
"Sales Management" -- ITT, Lynchburg, Virginia
"Motivating People" -- ITT, Portland, Oregon
"Time Management" -- ITT, Miami, Florida
"Working with Government" -- Southwestern Region Conference, IEEE, Phoenix, Arizona
"Technical Writing" -- Southwestern Region Conference, IEEE, Dallas, Texas

REFERENCES
Available upon request.

Peter Arneson

P.O. Box 74 • Savannah, GA 31432 • 912-555-3458 • arneson@xxx.com

OBJECTIVE

Environmental scientist position with emphasis on microenvironmental design.

RELEVANT EXPERIENCE AND ACCOMPLISHMENTS

- In large multistate energy corporation, ensure all departmental units are in compliance with CERCLA in terms of releases to air, water, or soil; SARA; and TSCA (PCBs). Also, verify all purchased products appear on the EPA TSCA Inventory.

- Ensure compliance with RCRA for hazardous waste disposal for hazardous waste landfill operation and maintain compliance with Small Quantity Generator Requirements.

- Organize Environmental Compliance Assessment Reviews of all branch operations and departments to review permits, records, training, and compliance in the field.

- Developed environmental compliance programs, drainage control programs, and waste disposal/minimization programs.

- Supervised installation of ozone-generating machines at various plants for treating water used underground for dust suppression.

- Investigated use of ozone for cyanide destruction in a heap leach, drinking water treatment, coal preparation, and sanitary waste treatment.

- Developed inexpensive and efficient method of destroying outer membrane of *T. ferroxxidans* bacteria, which produces acid on coal refuse.

EMPLOYMENT HISTORY

- Environmental Scientist, Webco Power, Inc., Savannah, GA, 2000–present
- Research Scientist, General Electric Corp., Columbia, MO, 1997–2000
- Research Technician, Georgia Institute of Technology, Atlanta, GA, 1993–1997

EDUCATION

M.S., Environmental Science, University of Missouri, Columbia, 2000
Special emphasis on microenvironmental design.

B.S., Agriculture, Georgia Institute of Technology, Atlanta, 1993

M A R C U S   G .   H A I N E S

P.O. Box 234 • Saginaw, MI 48603 • (517) 555-4438

E X P E R I E N C E   S U M M A R Y

More than seven years of varied hydrogeologic experience in performing and managing remedial investigations and environmental assessments. Associated with RCRA corrective actions, NPL and Michigan State Superfund sites, landfill closures, property transfers, and mining operations.

E D U C A T I O N

M.S., Geology, Oregon State University, Corvallis, 1983
Minor in Environmental Science and Hydrology
B.A., Geology, Shawnee State University, Portsmouth, OH, 1980

E X P E R I E N C E / K E Y   P R O J E C T S

- Supervised a multiphased hydrogeologic investigation as part of RCRA corrective action provisions at a U.S. Department of Defense facility. Prepared work plan and oversaw field activities, budget tracking, field investigation reports, and final RCRA Facility Investigation Report.
- Led remedial investigation (RI) at a Superfund site outside Milwaukee, Wisconsin, as field team leader. Designed, implemented, and managed the following field programs: surface water/sediment sampling, air sampling, bioassay sampling, drilling, groundwater sampling, packer tests, test pit excavation, and surveying. Prepared four RI reports.
- Performed numerous Phase I environmental liability assessments and subsequent Phase II hydrogeologic investigations for property transfers in several states.
- Supervised a hydrogeologic investigation as part of a Phase II environmental liability assessment in Edwardsville, Illinois. Monitored well installation, sampled groundwater, prepared summary report, and tracked project budget.
- Implemented various phases of hydrogeologic investigations, including drilling supervision, monitoring well installation, groundwater sampling, aquifer testing, geophysical surveys, air monitoring, writing investigation reports, and assisting with topographic surveys for geoscience corporation.

E M P L O Y M E N T

- Geoscientist, Markham Environmental Engineering Corp., Saginaw, MI, 1999 to present
- Staff Geologist, Sorrel Geoscience Corp., Pittsburgh, PA, 1993 to 1999

P R O F E S S I O N A L   M E M B E R S H I P S /   A F F I L I A T I O N S

AIPG Certified Geologist
Member, Association of Groundwater Scientists and Engineers
Certified Professional Geologist

R E F E R E N C E S

Available upon request

Evelyn Tickell

4978 Broadway • Boulder, Colorado 80304 • 303-555-3892

Objective

To obtain a position as a high school science or environmental studies teacher.

Education

University of Colorado, Boulder, CO, Teaching Certification, grades 1–12, 2002
Colorado State University, Fort Collins, CO, Bachelor of Science, Zoology, 1977

Professional Experience

Instructor, Boulder County Environmental Education Center, Boulder, CO
Instructed classes in zoology and environmental ecology, including plant and tree identification, using classroom and outdoor hands-on techniques. Supervised overnight trips for high school students. Developed and wrote booklet on endangered Colorado wildlife for use as textbook. Volunteer, part-time staff, 2002–present.

Consultant, Pokahu Ranch, Maui, HI
Developed and wrote a conservation plan for the protection and restoration of the native ecosystem. Researched and evaluated the natural history recovery plans, regulations, and recommendations of government officials. Performed species counts and determined the possibilities of rehabilitation of disturbed lands, eradication of pests, and reintroduction of endangered species. April–June 2000.

Biological Assistant, University of Colorado Wildlife Department, Boulder, CO
Participated in capture, tagging, and relocation of bighorn sheep in Colorado, and in dietary studies of large ungulates. Assisted in research of black-capped chickadees: made sonogram recordings, maintained 75 birds. Took part in research of endangered fish species in western Colorado rivers: collected fish, identified species, collected data, performed literature search, and compiled and condensed information. 1999–2000.

Scientific Technician, Washington State Department of Fisheries, Olympia, WA
Assisted in biological studies to assess the use of natural and artificial habitats by marine fish species to developed criteria for habitat protection, mitigation, and enhancement. Collected and compiled data on salmonids for habitat protection and harvest management purposes, including species identification, length, weight, scale sampling, sex, mark sampling, tagging, and redd (salmon spawning "nests") identification. Identified marine micro-invertebrates for fish stomach analysis. Performed surveys of herring and smelt spawn, plankton tows, and beach seines, and took eelgrass samples. Interviewed sport and commercial fishers. Prepared data summaries, charts, illustrations, and graphs. Various departments, 1977–1999.

References provided upon request.

Jean K. Schumann

389 SW 13th Avenue   Olympia, WA 97301   206-555-3982

CAREER OBJECTIVE
To obtain a position as Scientific Technician for the Washington Department of Fisheries or the U.S. Department of Natural Resources.

SUMMARY OF EXPERIENCE
- Collected biological data as Biological Aide at Washington Coastal Aquarium.
- Participated in field study emphasizing terrestrial vegetation, geological features, and marine organisms, and maintained field journal of activities, including transect and plot studies.
- Participated in compiling environmental report for county subarea plan, producing vegetation map, writing and editing sections of report, and presenting group results to planning committee.
- Maintained records of shipments, collected and prepared ore samples for chemical analysis, and assisted in surveying.
- Developed and implemented marine biology programs (Intertidal Organisms and Cobbled Shore Habitat) along with a cultural history program for use at Girl Scout camps.
- Assisted in supervising and training staff, planning programs, and evaluating performance of marine biology and cultural history programs.
- Taught and led nature activities for children and adults in marine and terrestrial biology, intertidal habitats and organisms, forest ecosystems, botany, zoology, and meteorology.
- Supervised trip planning and taught skills in equipment use, map reading, fire making, shelter building, and minimum-impact camping.

WORK HISTORY
- Community Resource Staff, Campus Recreation Center, Deschutes University, Olympia, WA, 1995 - present.
- Assistant Director, Program Planner, Rainier Girl Scout Council, Tacoma, WA, 1990 - 1995.
- Program Development Intern, Rainier Girl Scout Council, Tacoma, WA, 1989.
- Biological Aide, Washington Coast Aquarium, Long Beach, WA, summers, 1985 - 1989.
- Biological Assistant, Taber Shipments, Inc., Spokane, WA, 1984.

EDUCATION
Deschutes University, Olympia, WA, 1989.
   Bachelor of Arts in Environmental Education
   Bachelor of Science in Biology

REFERENCES AVAILABLE ON REQUEST.

SEAN PETER MICHAELS

443 Fairway Court
Cheboygan, Michigan 49721
616-555-2983

OBJECTIVE

A position as technical writer for a consulting company or research group

SUMMARY OF SKILLS

- Experienced and trained in technical writing
- Expert in wildlife biology, fisheries biology, policy and implementation; also knowledgeable about other technical fields
- Computer experience: IBM and Macintosh, Microsoft Word, Excel, and Power-Point; Harvard Graphics; Professional Write; Lotus 1-2-3; Pascal; SAS (statistical analysis)

EDUCATION

- Coursework in Technical Writing and Editing, University of Michigan, Ann Arbor, 2001-2002
- B.S., Fisheries and Wildlife Management, University of Maine, Orono, 1980

PROFESSIONAL EXPERIENCE

Wildlife Biologist, Blue Water Wetlands Center, Cheboygan, Michigan
1995-present

- Document spring migration of water birds and raptors. Coordinate breeding bird counts and banding efforts. Coordinate 5 to 15 technicians and 20 volunteers who assist in gathering data. Write annual technical report that describes methods, summarizes results, and discusses the documentation of migrating wetlands birds. Analyze trends in species increase or decrease over time. Assist in producing Blue Water's quarterly newsletter. Write lay articles for the newsletter.

Wildlife Technician, U.S. Department of Natural Resources, Alaska
1990-1995

- Assisted in study comparing habitat use selection by pine marten in three post-fire successive stages. Participated in aerial telemetry; live-trapped marten and small mammals; managed databases; assisted in writing, editing, and proofreading annual reports.

Wildlife Technician, University of Maine, Orono
1982-1989
- Assisted in M.S. research project investigating the relationship between bird species richness and forest clear-cut size and assessing nest predation frequency with distance to clear-cut edge. Identified avian species by sight and sound; placed and investigated artificial bird nests; mist-netted and banded migratory songbirds.
- Participated in Ph.D. research project investigating the relationship between beaver-created wetlands and waterfowl density. Censused breeding pairs of waterfowl and nongame species; constructed and installed water-damage control devices; live-trapped, sexed, anesthetized, and tagged beaver.
- Assisted in an interdisciplinary study to assess the impact of airborne pollutants of a coastal red spruce ecosystem. Prepared, maintained, and constructed atmospheric monitoring equipment; collected and prepared foliar tissue for elemental analysis.

Research Assistant, Holt Research Forest, Arrowsic, Maine
1980-1982
- Assisted in an intensive biomonitoring study of a diverse forested ecosystem. Analyzed forest structure; identified vegetation; trapped small mammals; collected and entered data.

OTHER RELEVANT EXPERIENCE

Maine Forester Yearbook: Assistant Photography Editor
The Wildlife Society: Wood duck box maintenance.
Boy Scouts of America: Eagle Scout and Order of the Arrow

PROFESSIONAL MEMBERSHIPS

National Association of Science Writers, Northeast Chapter
The Wildlife Society
The Wildlife Society—Maine Student Chapter
National Wildlife Federation
The Nature Conservancy

Writing portfolio and references available on request

Charles Andawa

4783 West Maple
Baltimore, MD 21233
Cellular phone: (301) 555-2983
E-mail: CharlesAndawa@xxx.com

Objective

To obtain a position in Chemical Engineering with an environmental engineering organization.

Experience

1998-present
Senior Project Manager, PPD, Inc., Baltimore, MD
- Supervise thirty-two employees. Direct, supervise, administer, and manage several projects from inception to start-up, including new chemical process equipment manufacturing. Assist Sales Department in reviewing the system process design, scheduling, engineering, and costs before final proposal is presented to client.
- Conceived, initiated, and developed chemical formations for nontoxic solutions used for oil recovery and recycling. Formulated empirical equations and design criteria for the system, which resulted in increasing company sales sevenfold over the last five years.
- Instituted procedures for project document handling, filing, and project communication, including project status summaries to management and clients.
- Trained project engineers and project managers to design and manage projects.
- Participated in developing service-system study concept to introduce PPD's name into new markets, which increased sales by 50 percent in that market.

1984-1998
Senior Project and Process Engineer, Moreland Chemical, Annapolis, MD
- Planned, scheduled, developed process design, and wrote specifications for major projects, including pulp liquor evaporation system operations, sand reclamation systems, waste wood utilization to manufacture charcoal, sewage sludge oxidation, waste oxidation, and heat recovery.
- Held complete process and project responsibility of four projects from proposal stage through plant start-up, including budgeting. Supervised 23 chemical and physical engineers and laboratory technicians.

Page 1 of 2

1982-1984
Process and Plant Engineer, Cecero's, Inc., Annapolis, MD
- Assumed responsibility for chemical plant troubleshooting; process studies; process development; project cost estimation; equipment design; and equipment sizing, selection, and purchasing.
- Oversaw utility optimization, air and water pollution controls, boiler operations, and incinerator operations.
- Coordinated plant work with Production Department.

1979-1982
Process Development Engineer, U.S. Chemical Co., Philadelphia, PA
- Worked on solvent exchange and through-air drying of tissue paper.
- Operated high speed pacer machine to test through-air drying concept.

Education

1979, B.S., M.S., Chemical Engineering, Minnesota Technical University, Houghton

References

Available upon request.

Yoshio Umeki

9783 Ridgeway Drive
Evanston, IL 60204
708-555-2983
umeki@xxx.com

Objective
A position as Publicist for an environmental agency

Summary of Qualifications
* Seven years of experience writing on environmental issues
* Thorough knowledge of environmental issues and regulations
* Excellent connections within the government agencies concerned with the environment
* Skilled at working with the public
* Experienced and published writer
* Accustomed to working with deadlines
* Flexible and hardworking
* Knowledgeable about local government, business, and community

History of Employment
News Reporter, *Chicago Tribune*, 1997-present.
* Specialize in environmental news. Complete assignments and research leads.
* Interview local government officials, corporate officers, community activists, and business owners. Developed the series "Up in Smoke" detailing emissions reports for ten major factories; resulted in tighter regulations for the city of Chicago as well as a Benny Award for investigative journalism. Developed a five-part series exploring community relations of Illinois businesses.

Education Reporter, *Honolulu Star-Bulletin*, 1981-1997.
* Started as proofreader and within a year had written several feature stories. Obtained responsibility to research and report all education news within two years.

Selected List of Publications
"Up in Smoke: What's Really Coming out of Those Smokestacks?"
"Hadley & Hadley's Scramble for Community Support"
"Community Coalition: A Homegrown Response to Environmental Waste"
"Volunteerism: A Way of Life at Wright Brothers"
"Hawaii's Schools: Rebuilding Promises"
"Amelia Hunani: A New Breed of Administrator"
"Evanston's Four-Story Community: A Look at North Broadway"
"Revitalization: How Upscaling Affects Uptown Residents"
"WESTSTAR's Model Environmental Enrichment Program"

Education
B.A. in Journalism and Government, University of Hawaii, Honolulu, 1980

References and publication portfolio on request

Merika P. Hayes

3892 Birdseye Lane • Topeka, Kansas 66603 • 803-555-9382

Objective

A position teaching environmental education to children

Education

Candidate, M.E., Kansas City College, Kansas
1995–1999, courses in educational theory, literacy

B.S., University of Iowa
1995, Environmental Science

Work Experience

Instructor, Echo Mountain Outdoor School, Maryland
March–September 1995–2001

Taught groups of schoolchildren in an overnight environmental education program. Assisted in developing curriculum. Taught hands-on classes in local ponds, woods, swamps, and Chesapeake Bay. Taught survival skills and rope course initiatives. Supervised children 24 hours a day during each three-to-five-day stay at the school.

Tutor, University of Iowa, Iowa City
1993–1995

Tutored biology and chemistry in school-based tutorial program. Tutored individuals and small groups in biology and chemistry, focusing on problem solving.

Seasonal Naturalist, Corkscrew Swamp Sanctuary, National Audubon Society, Georgia
Summer 1994

Interpreted natural history, including group walks and demonstrations, hikes, and vehicular treks. Answered questions along boardwalk trails. Created formal presentations. Staffed visitor center. Maintained trail and grounds. Participated in land management activities.

Intern, Francis Markum Forest, Ohio
June–November, 1993

Participated in many facets of running a nature sanctuary. Led interpretive talks/walks. Staffed nature center. Completed wildlife research. Collected and collated data. Monitored acid rain levels. Assisted in basic maintenance of buildings and grounds.

Memberships

National Wildlife Federation, Greenpeace, National Audubon Society

Volunteer Experience

Teacher's aide, Pearson Elementary School, Topeka, Kansas
Photographer, Topeka Birder's Alliance

Lucina Alvarez

1283 Bramble Drive   (512) 555-1707 home
Austin, TX 78710   (512) 555-3602 office

Objective
To obtain a position as senior technical editor for a large environmental agency or publisher.

Education
Columbia University. M.A., English. GPA, 3.91 -- 1997.
Columbia University. B.A. with Distinction, Phi Beta Kappa, English with Creative Writing Emphasis -- 1980.

Experience
Proposal Writer, Corporate and Foundation Relations
University of Texas Office of Development, Austin, TX
1995 to present
- Assist administrators and faculty in writing and editing a broad range of grant proposals for technical and lay audiences.
- Develop, write, and design public relations and fund-raising materials for the university's maximum-priority projects. Review annual reports and other corporate publications to identify major donor prospects.
- Conduct quarterly seminars for staff and faculty on proposal writing. Supervise student assistant. Involvement in generating gifts to the university totaling over $3.1 million during first year.

Board of Directors, Fund-Raising Chair
Wild Rose Press, Austin, TX
1998 to present
- Hold volunteer administrative and fund-raising responsibilities for small nonprofit literary press.
- Write and edit grant proposals to government agencies and private foundations.

Freelance Writer, Graphic Designer, and Photographer
Austin, TX
1990 to present
- Provide services including color and black-and-white photography; desktop publishing; writing and editing newsletters, catalogs, advertisements, feature articles, and public relations materials. Recently researched and wrote science biographies for technical reference book.

Page 1 of 2

Promotions Assistant
University Book Stores, Inc., Austin, TX
1985 to 1995

- Wrote, designed, and produced store brochures, flyers, signs, and advertisements. Mastered desktop publishing, graphics, and production methods.

Program Manager and Events Coordinator
Drake's Books & Magazines, New York, NY
1980 to 1984

- Assumed responsibility for public relations and all aspects of weekly reading series at NYC's third-largest independent bookseller.
- Designed and wrote all advertising copy, press releases, catalogs, brochures, and employee training manuals.
- Scheduled author appearances and hosted and introduced authors at events with audiences ranging from 50 to 400, including Pulitzer Prize-winners Taylor Branch and Tracy Kidder and National Book Award-winner Stephen Jay Gould.
- Supervised a staff of two.

Other Skills

Expertise in Microsoft Office 2000 and many other MS/DOS and Macintosh word processing, desktop publishing, and graphics programs.

Recent Publications

June 2001 -- *The New War: Forests vs. Lumber*, Austin Press, Austin, TX.
February 2001 -- "John Hope," *The Nobel Prize Winners: Physiology and Medicine*, Austin Press, Austin, TX.
February 2001 -- "Miles Horne," *The Nobel Prize Winners: Physiology and Medicine*, Austin Press, Austin, TX.

Completed Manuscripts

March 2002 -- "On the Road with Aaron Cross, Environmentalist Extraordinaire," for *American Environmentalist*.
December 2001 -- *Understanding Media*, with Lyle, Roberts, Sherry Huber, and Alice Barker.

Memberships

Phi Beta Kappa
Council for the Advancement and Support of Education
National Society of Fund-Raising Executives

Current References and Writing Sample

Available upon request.

J. William Clark

4437 White Oaks Drive
Urbana, IL 61801
Daytime (217) 555-2847
Evening (217) 555-3345

Objective

An executive position in an organization involved with environmental public policy

Professional Experience

Executive Consultant, Social Policy and Study Center
George Washington University, Washington, D.C., 1984 to 2001
  Developed and taught seminars on organizational management and global economic and environmental issues in business for officials from the governments of 14 countries. Coordinated the development of an environmental protection plan for a major public policy research organization. Represented senior management with the government auditing agency requiring the environmental plan. Advised the Economic Policy Research Institute, the Sierra Club, and W. W. Group International, an organization that monitors and analyzes environmental public policy issues throughout the world.

Lecturer, Management and Public Administration
Graduate Center, University of Illinois, Urbana-Champaign, 1978 to 1984
  Taught organizational management courses for the College of Commerce and Business Administration, including Managing Organizations (process of organizing, planning, and controlling), Organizational Behavior (leadership, internal politics, and group dynamics), The Global Business Environment (domestic and international political, economic, and social issues that affect complex organizations), and Public Policy Administration (development, structure, and implementation of public policy).

Assistant Executive Director, National School Boards Association
Washington, D.C., and Chicago, IL, 1973 to 1978
> Planned, organized, developed, and coordinated programs and activities for the national network of school district trustees from the nation's urban centers. Consulted with the director of the President's Commission on School Finance, the executive director of the Education Commission of the States, and the National Advisory Committee on Career Education.

Program Associate, National Public Schools Support Association
Washington, D.C., 1970 to 1973
> Held full financial accountability for budgeting, planning, controlling, and personnel management. Provided consulting services to school districts and support organizations nationally.

> Previous employment includes three years as a public school teacher in Illinois and four years active duty as an officer in the U.S. Navy.

Education

Ph.D., Politics and Public Policy Administration
George Washington University, 1977

M.B.A., Finance and Administration
Purdue University, 1970

B.A., Business and Economics (Naval ROTC)
Purdue University, 1965

Memberships

National Field Task Force for the Preservation and Protection of American Resources, U.S. Department of Agriculture

Retired Naval Reserve Officers Association

References on request

Faith Nuygen

775 SW Tilbury Road • Fresno, California 93723
(209) 555-7623 • Nuygen@xxx.com

Experience

Risk Manager, Consortium of California Counties, Fresno
1993 - present

Develop and implement risk management system to assure limitation of program risks and compliance with federal and state laws. Serve as liaison to district branch offices and state, regional, and federal offices of the Department of Agriculture in the interpretation and implementation of environmental laws and regulations.

- Develop system of procedures to identify and monitor program risks.
- Conduct comprehensive risk management reviews of districts for compliance with state and federal laws.
- Assume responsibility for development, training, and implementation of policy and statewide environmental action plan. Investigate and process public complaints.
- Developed emergency response procedure and trained all local government safety managers statewide.

Communications Manager, Consortium of California Counties, Fresno
1986 - 1993

Administered an annual federal grant of $25 million for employment and training programs in 35 counties for the consortium. Developed and implemented a public relations effort for the Job Training Partnership Act (JTPA) as the first Communications Manager of the Administrative Office.

- Developed annual report, newsletter, brochures, and other materials to market program's job training services to private business, public sector, and job seekers.
- Received National Business Alliance Distinguished Performance Award.
- Conceived and managed a statewide conference for employment and training professionals; hosted visiting International Fellowship representatives from four European countries.
- Coordinated communications among various branches and government offices.

- Designed and maintained systems for recruiting, selecting, and training members of the Private Industry Association of California and local elected officials of the CCC Board of Directors. Managed quarterly meetings and biannual retreat.
- Coordinated multimedia job seeker recruitment campaign sold in 26 states.
- Tracked state and federal legislation with potential impact on CCC programs. Prepared testimony and information for legislators. Attended state legislative hearings.

Personnel Director, International Paper Suppliers, San Francisco, California
1982 - 1986

Carried out industrial relations functions and monitored EEO/AA activities for a corporation with 95 locations nationwide as the first woman in the corporation's history to hold this position.

- Interpreted and administered labor contract and represented the company in local and master bargaining.
- Developed corporate policy manual on EEO/AA. Designed a brochure for corporate use and conducted regional EEO/AA seminars in corporate supervisory training courses.
- Coordinated corporate community programs.
- Worked with field managers to prepare for government regulations compliance review.

Education
B.A. in Communications, Stanford University, 1978

Portfolio and references available on request.

Anthony Wyatt

3892 Main Street #485 • Fairbanks, Alaska 99704 • 907-555 3398

Objective

A challenging position as media liaison for an organization dedicated to the protection of native fish and wildlife.

Work Experience

- **Host, writer, and producer** of the nationally syndicated "Fishing Line" radio program, which has been syndicated to 100 radio stations since 1999. Perform all phases of research. Establish contacts in person, by mail, and by phone. Oversee all aspects of creation and electronic production of 1/4-inch master audiotapes. 1995-present.
- **Public relations, marketing coordinator** for Fishing Line Communications Network. Provided affiliate radio station PR service via phone, mail, or personal appearance. Assisted in locating suitable corporate sponsors and convincing them of the merit of advertising via the network. 1991-1995.
- **Reporter, news anchor, talk show host, disc jockey, commercial producer, announcer, editor** for KCLA-FM, KRDD-FM, KFLY AM-FM-TV, KSKY-FM, KPKR-AM, and KPBB-FM, Anchorage Public Radio. 1982-1990.
- **Instructor**, Broadcast Arts, Ronald Pembroke School of Broadcast, Pilsberg University, New York. Presented formal classroom lectures, chalk-talks, equipment demonstrations, and guidance for classes in copywriting, newswriting, interviewing, editing, and production. 1987-1990.

Publications

- *Salmon Fishing in Alaska and the Northwest Territories*, published 2002, Binns & Finkley, New York.
- *Outside Air*, circulation 8,000, monthly column, State of Alaska.
- *Fishing the Atlantic Salmon*, published 1990, Binns & Finkley, New York.
- "Backpacking for Adirondack Trout," *Fishing Adventures Magazine*, spring 1990.
- "Brook Trout Fishing in Upstate New York," *Fishing Adventures Magazine*, fall 1987.

Education

Coursework toward Master of Arts in Communications (36 credits), New York State, 2001-2002.
B.A. in Broadcast Journalism, Pilsberg University, Albany, New York, 1982.

References

Available upon request.

JEAN HANAKA

3829 Deering Street, Apt. 23A • Portland, Maine 04101
207-555-2483 • Hanaka12@xxx.com

• Objective

A position as wildlife photographer for a major wildlife protection agency or organization.

• Education

B.F.A., Photography, New England Institute of Art, Maine, 2002.

Coursework in Art and Photography, South Central Community College, Buffalo, New York, 1980-1981.

B.S., Wildlife Biology, Plainfield College, Plainfield, Vermont, 1979.

• Professional Experience

1991-present, Staff Photographer/Publications Coordinator
Community Relations Office, University of Southern Maine, Portland
Coordinate photographic coverage and take photographs for campus events and organizations. Produce educational and promotional material (copy and photos) for many campus events and displays, both on and off campus. Write advertising copy for both radio and newspapers. Design and assist in designing advertising layout for newspapers. Establish and reorganize procedures for maintaining records, billings, and follow-up. Organize detailed record-keeping for the Speaker's Service. Initiate surveys and tabulation of area rental rooms, prices, and contact persons. Write office guidelines, including an office procedures manual. Maintain campus maps, staff directory, and new employee packets. Monitor and assign work to four classified staff and supervise three to six work-study students.

1989-1991, Staff Photographer
Learning Resource Center, Buffalo, New York
Provided photographs for *LRC Newsletter*, biannual bulletin, and promotion and publicity use. Researched community events, local news, and trends for news and photography leads. Attended all Learning Resource Center events. Completed layouts of newsletter and bulletin.

1981-1989, Senior Secretary
Community Relations Office, University of Southern Maine, Portland
Assisted the community relations director. Maintained office records. Coordinated room reservations, Speaker's Service functions, and assignments for the graphics area.

Portfolio of wildlife photos and references available upon request.

Susan L. Jeffers

2235 SW Hammond
Laramie, Wyoming 82057
Cell: (307) 555-9872

Career Goal

Communications Director for an environmental consulting organization.

Demonstrated Skills

- Marketing and public relations—developing marketing strategies and campaigns, dealing with sensitive issues with the news media, and developing and projecting an organization's most positive image.
- Ability to develop plans, goals, strategies, and timelines, and to maintain schedules and analyze the results of projects.
- Ability to work independently and exercise sound judgment.
- Excellent communications skills, both in writing and in making public presentations to small and large groups on a variety of topics.
- Ability to work effectively with the public, elected officials, board and committee members, program operators, and staff in a team environment.
- Grant writing and fund-raising.
- Thorough knowledge of state and federal government operations and regulations affecting business in the state.
- Preparation and production of graphics materials, including brochures, newsletters, and annual reports.
- Knowledge of newspaper advertising department practices in advertising sales, placement, and design.

Professional Experience

Special Topics Researcher: Environment, Education, Public Policy, *Laramie Evening News*, Wyoming, January 1998 to present

Research Specialist, Public Relations Department, State of Wyoming, June 1992 to 1998

Advertising Production, *Sheridan Sun*, Wyoming, August 1988 to November 1991

Advertising Intern, *Laramie Evening News*, Wyoming, June 1988 to August 1988

Education

B.A. in Journalism/Advertising, University of Wyoming, Laramie, 1988
    AASA award for design of print advertising campaign.

Gavin McCloud

P.O. Box 12   St. Paul, MN 53402   Cellular: 612-555-0932   Gavin@xxx.com

Objective
A position as a high school environmental science/ecology teacher

Education
University of Minnesota, Minneapolis, Master of Education, 2002
University of Vermont, Burlington, Bachelor of Science—Biology, 1976

Professional Certification
Minnesota: Elementary, 1–6
Minnesota: Middle and High School, 7–12

Related Skills and Experience
➤ Taught classes in stream ecology, outdoor survival, backpacking, and trip planning. Supervised overnight trips for primary and secondary school students. Assisted in developing programs and designing courses aimed at integrating science education with outdoor activities.
➤ Assisted in research on stream ecology and effects of pollutants: collected samples and other data, performed literature searches, and compiled and condensed information.
➤ Also prepared data summaries, charts, illustrations, and graphs; wrote summary reports; evaluated methods, procedures, and results of stream ecology studies.
➤ Assisted in biological studies to assess natural and artificial habitats of woodland species for developing habitat protection, mitigation, and enhancement criteria: collected data on weasel population for habitat protection purposes; participated in capture, tagging, and monitoring of small mammals.

Employment History
Instructor, Minnesota Outdoor Center, St. Paul, part-time staff, 1998–present

Biological Assistant, University of Minnesota Wildlife Department, Minneapolis, 1999–2000

Biological Assistant, State of Minnesota Department of Wildlife, St. Paul, various departments, 1977–1999

References
Available upon request

Hank Lee Talbot

1770 Meter Road
Wilmington, NC 28403
Cellular: 919-555-0656
Hank.Talbot@xxx.com

Objective: A research or field assistantship in international ecological studies

Education: University of North Carolina, Wilmington
Bachelor of Science in Biology and Ecological Systems, 2000
Relevant courses: Population Ecology, Wildlife Biology, Animal Behavior, Biochemistry, Developmental Biology, Comparative Anatomy, Animal Nutrition, General Chemistry, Inorganic Chemistry, Organic Chemistry

Experience: Coastal Animal Hospital, Wilmington, NC
summers, 1996-2000
Veterinarian's assistant

School of Field Research, Lake Victoria, Kenya
Ecology Semester, fall 1999
Studied land-use issues facing developing countries in attempting to preserve natural wildlife.
Conducted population research on scavenger birds through a capture and mark program for marabou storks and white-backed vultures.

Ecological Independent Study, Wilmington, NC
Spring 1999
Studied the effect of natural disturbances on pine and cedar trees by correlating changes in cover with juvenile growth.

Service: Assistant at Beverly Cronin Home for Senior Citizens, 1996-present
CROP Hunger Awareness, 1996-present
Campus Recycling, 1996-2000

References available upon request

KEN LU HON

3890 Piedmont Drive ■ Arlington, MA 02174 ■ (617) 555-3928

■ OBJECTIVE

Research scientist with a fisheries laboratory, investigating disease identification, prevention, and protection among salmonid species.

■ EDUCATION

1990 M.S., Fisheries Biology, Massachusetts Maritime Academy, Buzzards Bay
1983 B.S., Biology, University of Washington, Seattle

■ WORK HISTORY

1998–2002 **Research Scientist**
Massachusetts Cooperative Wildlife Research Unit
Studied food selection and foraging tactics of sea otters and their relationship to decline in fisheries industry on the Atlantic coast. Prepared government policy report and recommendations.

1992–98 **Fishery Technician**
Massachusetts Department of Fish and Game
Studied selected vertebrate endangered species off the Atlantic coast of the United States. Tracked migrating species to determine effects of shipping industry, fisheries, and predators on sustained habitat.

1985–92 **Limnology Lab Assistant**
Washington Department of Fisheries and Wildlife
Identified and classified various saltwater species of invertebrates. Worked on project to chart feeding characteristics of sea otter populations off the Pacific coastline in Washington, Oregon, and northern California.

■ OTHER TRAINING

1983 Beginning SCUBA diving, University of Washington
1982 Basic SCUBA diving, National Association of Underwater Instructors (NAUI)

■ MEMBERSHIPS

Marine Mammal Society (Charter Member)
American Ornithologists' Union
American Fisheries Society (Regional Vice President)

References, list of publications, and curriculum vita provided on request.

janelle wilson

15987 South Barkley • Oklahoma City, Oklahoma 73123
(226) 555-6799 • E-mail: Janelle.Wilson@xxx.com

Objective
Position as Environmental Engineer with large regional organization.

Work Experience
Environmental Engineer
H.W. Bittner, Inc.
August 2000 - present
- Prepare environmental assessments and checklists, noise-level predictions, ambient noise levels.
- Advise design engineering on environmental problems, design cross sections, estimate construction quantities.
- Compute wetland involvement.

Utilities Relocation Engineer
Oklahoma State Department of Transportation
April 1996 - August 2000
- Worked with public utilities to relocate facilities within public right-of-way.
- Coordinated movement and developed movement agreements.
- Enforced clear zone.

Environmental Engineer
Oklahoma State Department of Transportation
January 1992 - March 1996
- Coordinated, reviewed, revised, and processed U.S. Army Corps of Engineer permits, shorelines, flood plains, and hydraulic permits.
- Prepared environmental checklists, impact statements, noise-level predictions, ambient noise levels, and air-level pollution levels. Investigated and advised for hazardous material spills, underground storage tanks, and site assessments.
- Prepared displays for public and court meetings. Reviewed environmental documents and permits; interpreted noise levels on projects and designed noise barriers; monitored and collected data on air quality.
- Reviewed and approved large lots, short plats, and roadway approaches for private developers.
- Assembled and calibrated nine air quality-control sets valued at $175,000 each.

Education
1992   M.S. Engineering, Oklahoma State University.
1991   B.S. Environmental Sciences, Oklahoma State University.

References available by request.

Aaron Williamson

P.O. Box W2354 • Grand Forks, North Dakota 58202
Awilliamson@xxx.com • Cellular: (701) 555-3452

General Qualifications

Served as SEPA-NEPA environmental geologist for over fourteen years for North Dakota State Department of Transportation (NDSDOT) projects. Completed assessments, air quality, noise-level surveys, permitting, and environmental projects. Conducted surveys and projected noise-level surveys. Wrote major portions of the department's many environmental assessments and environmental checklists. Determined wetland involvement prior to 1997. Coordinated all state, federal, and local permits (according to NEPA and SEPA requirements), and coordinated and negotiated for mitigation. Investigated for hazardous waste occurrence.

Screened NDSDOT district projects for eight years for archaeological and historical significance and contracted for evaluation services. Served as coordinator for the District Interdisciplinary Team. Formed NDSDOT district environmental department in 1984 and was self-supervised for over six years.

Worked as highway geologist for five years for foundation investigation, route survey, and sensitive geological areas. Also solved water-source pollution and correction as well as landslide investigation and correction problems.

Experience

Current title: District Geologist -- June 1989 to present (Other positions held during this period: Geologist I, II; Senior Geologist) North Dakota State Department of Transportation, Grand Forks

Conduct geological evaluation of state roads; identify and investigate soil types, landslide corrections, and construction materials. Test-drill; sample and test aggregate. Operate drilling equipment, solve hydrology complaints, write geological and soil reports. Correct landslide activities, perform hazardous waste investigations, and seek remedial action.

Education and Training

Environmental Assessment Site -- 2000
80-Hour Hazardous Waste Handler's Certificate, U.S. Environmental Protection Agency -- 2000
Miscellaneous Basic Computer Courses, NDSDOT -- 1996
Environmental Workshops -- 1995, 1996
Underground Storage Tank Removal Certificate -- 1995
Water Quality Research Workshop, University of North Dakota -- 1993
University of North Dakota, Secondary Certificate -- 1992
Acoustic Seminar, NDSDOT -- 1990
Noise, Highway Traffic, and Fundamentals, NDSDOT -- 1989
University of North Dakota, Bachelor of Science (Geology) -- 1989

References

Available upon request

Joanna Cassidy

2287 SW 29th Place
Savannah, GA 31406
(912) 555-4986
joanna.cassidy@xxx.com

Objective

Product development team position with an environmental manufacturing company.

Relevant Professional Experience

Southern Environmental Systems, Inc., Savannah, GA
Regional Manager
1999 to present
Manage development and sales of TELFABS high density polyethylene, structural geogrids, and other geosynthetic products for waste containment applications. Generated over $10,000,000 in new business.

Chemical Waste Management, Inc., Savannah, GA
Environmental Project Manager
1997 to 1998
Developed new business involving hazardous waste remedial services with targeted industries and operations throughout the Pacific Northwest.
1983 to 1986

Georgia Pacific Corporation, Savannah, GA
Environmental Product Manager
1993 to 1996
Planned and implemented a sales/marketing program for GeoWeave spunbonded, nonwoven, geotextile fabrics for protection of impermeable synthetic membranes in ponds, reservoirs, and landfills. Generated over $3,000,000 in new business.

Education

M.S., Chemical Engineering, Texas Tech University, Lubbock, 1990
B.S., Chemistry, Methodist College, Fayetteville, NC, 1988

References and detailed work history available on request.

DONNA HARRISON

P.O. Box B235 • Louisville, KY 40231

502/555-9219 • D.Harrison@xxx.com

EXPERIENCE

General Manager
Water Treatment Division, City of Louisville, KY
2000 to present
• Manage water treatment of city with population of 300,000.

Director
Environmental Resources Corporation, Memphis, TN
1998 to 2000
• Managed business and its financing structure.
• Developed and implemented innovative technology for water treatment.

Engineering Manager
Geometric Enterprises, Lexington, KY
1994 to 1997
• Assumed increasing responsibilities in the sales, design, and execution of various projects under contract with the U.S. Environmental Protection Agency, primarily in the chemical plant and waste management areas.
• Evaluated a number of waste treatment facilities.

Industrial Process Control Consultant
Midwest Chemical Industries, Ltd., Frankfort, KY
1992 to 1994
• Undertook process control systems design responsibility for a number of minerals processing plants constructed by Midwest Chemical, including the preparation of specifications, serving as client liaison, purchasing equipment, and supervising installation and start-up.

EDUCATION

Masters of Business Administration -- 1998, University of Kentucky
Bachelor of Science -- 1992, University of Alberta
   Chemical Engineering, First Class honors (two years)

ADDITIONAL DATA

Professional Engineer -- States of Kentucky and Tennessee
Available to travel and relocate
References available on request

SHAWNA B. DAVIS

30266 Fraser Creek Drive
Vancouver, WA 98623
E-mail: shawna.davis@xxx.com
Tel: (206) 555-1930

OBJECTIVE

Project Manager and Environmental Project Engineer for industrial or municipal facility with focus on design, construction, and operation. Willing to relocate.

SUMMARY

In-depth design and project experience in the waste management field, including the design and operation of energy recovery and recycling processes in the chemical, mining, and iron and steel industries. Extensive experience with progressively greater responsibility in varied managerial, project engineering, and technical sales positions, with primary strengths in the areas of environmental technology, process equipment, industrial process control, engineering management, and written and verbal communications.

EXPERIENCE

President/General Manager -- 1996 to present
Waste Products Corporation, Vancouver, WA
Manage the commercial development and facility design for a newly developed technology that converts municipal solid waste into an inert, lightweight aggregate. Also took on a variety of consulting projects.

Chief Instrumentation Engineer/Project Engineer -- 1994 to 1996
Central Engineering Department, NACCO, Bellingham, WA
Coordinated the design, scheduling, and procurement activities for the preparation of feasibility studies for new mineral processing facilities in Australia and Indonesia. Supervised outside consultants and took numerous field trips to gather site and other relevant data.

Sales Supervisor/Project Engineer -- 1989 to 1994
Jenner & North, Inc., Seattle, WA
Sold and executed a number of major industrial automation projects, primarily in the mining, iron ore pelletizing, steel making, and power industries.

Page 1 of 2

Development Engineer -- 1983 to 1989
Taysom Engineering, Boise, ID
Coordinated owners, consultants, government planning agencies, contractors, and tenants on a number of commercial and industrial development projects.

EDUCATION

Master of Science degree, University of Washington, Seattle -- 1993
Civil Engineering for Environmental Management, Part-Time Executive Program

Bachelor of Science degree, University of Washington, Seattle -- 1983
Electrical Engineering, Honors

ADDITIONAL DATA

Member -- National Association of Environmental Professionals
Professional Engineer -- States of Washington, Idaho
Proficient in Microsoft Office 2000 and Lotus 1-2-3
Excellent oral and written communications
Proposal and business plan preparation experience

REFERENCES

Available upon request

Sonja Goldstein

2215 South Median Way • Reno, Nevada 89503

702-555-4498 • Goldstein1@xxx.com

Professional Objective

Seeking a management position emphasizing acquired skills, education, and experience in the environmental industry, including:

➤ General Management
➤ Personnel and Operations Management
➤ Financial Administration/Accounting
➤ Technical Management

Qualifications and Achievements

Over 15 years of executive-level management experience with primary emphasis and expertise in the following areas:

Operations Management

➤ Large, Complex, Project Direction, Coordination, and Definition
➤ Strategic Long- and Short-Range Planning
➤ Site Selection and Facilities/Plant Setup
➤ Property Acquisitions, Sales, and Disposition
➤ Market Research, Assessment, and Analysis

Personnel Management

➤ Personnel Recruitment and Performance Evaluation
➤ Salary Negotiation and Administration
➤ Fostering Creative, Cooperative, and Productive Employees
➤ Relationships in a Disciplined Work Environment

Financial Administration

➤ Budget Planning and Administration
➤ Initiation of Capitalization and Monitoring of Funding
➤ Financial Analysis and Reporting

Professional Experience

Nevada Department of Environmental Quality
Environmental Specialist -- Reno, Nevada, 1992 to present

➤ Conduct Superfund hazardous waste site preliminary assessments and site investigations.
➤ Monitor remediation activities and response actions; review technical, design, and other engineering documents.
➤ Regulate state and federal hazardous and solid-waste laws and regulations.

Page 1 of 2

Consultant
Independent Environmental Consultant -- Denver, Colorado, 1990 to 1992
➤ Served as the approved environmental contractor for the Resolution Trust Corporation.
➤ Acted as lead consultant for Water and Slurry Purification Processes, Inc. (WASPP), a water-quality remediation firm.

Division One Polymers, Inc.
Vice President and General Manager -- Denver, Colorado, 1988 to 1990
➤ Involved with initial capitalization effort, site selection, and facilities construction for this solid-waste recycling operation.
➤ Generated initial contacts for sales and recycling sources.
➤ Oversaw financial administration and strategic planning.

Consultant
Independent Business Consultant -- Denver, Colorado, 1986 to 1988
➤ Conducted business valuations, sales, and acquisitions: involved with environmental audits and potential liabilities.

Denver Oil Production Company
Senior Technical Advisor to the Region Staff -- Denver, Colorado, 1983 to 1986
➤ Monitored major drilling funds.
➤ Coordinated corporate lawsuit technical information.
➤ Assisted the corporate political lobby effort, including testimony in Washington, DC.

Geologist, Group Supervisor, Division Geologist -- 1973 to 1983
➤ Supervised three group leaders, and 28 professionals and support staff.
➤ Formulated budgets, salary administration policies, project definitions, and exploration strategies.

Education

University of Nevada, Las Vegas, Nevada -- B.S. in Geology, 1973

Colorado School of Mines, Golden, Colorado -- Completed intensive 11-week program on hazardous waste management in Department of Environmental Engineering, 1990

References Available Upon Request

Terrence W. Quentin

P.O. Box 125G   Montgomery, AL 36125   (205) 555-9842

Employment History

1991 to present   Environmental Consultant (Private)

1986 to 1991   Manager, Ecology and Contingency Plans for BP America, St. Louis, MO (Corporate Health, Safety, and Environmental Quality Department)

1983 to 1986   Associate Director, Institute of Urban Studies, Alabama State University; Environmental Scientist and Associate Professor of Biology and Health Sciences, Alabama State University (Tenured)

1979 to 1983   Assistant Professor of Biology, Alabama State University

Environmental Management Experience Summary

- Water Quality Management/Wastewater Treatment Systems
- Environmental Auditing as a Management Tool
- Environmental Regulatory Course Development and Training
- Hazardous Substance Inventories/Emissions Reporting
- Bioremediation/Hazardous Waste Management
- Aquatic Ecology/Environmental Toxicology
- Spill Prevention and Response
- Contingency Planning and Crisis Management
- Air Quality Modeling/Air Toxics
- Facility Hazard Analysis/Risk Assessment
- Land-Use Planning/Site Assessment
- Legislative and Regulatory Analysis/Lobbying
- Natural Resource Damage Assessment

Education

Ph.D. in Biology and Physiology, University of Georgia, 1979
B.S. and M.S. in Biology, Kennesaw State College, Marietta, GA, 1974, 1976

Numerous short courses in topics such as environmental law and regulations, oil and hazardous substance spill response, water-quality management, water-quality statistics and databases, industrial risk assessment, remote sensing and land-use planning, and business management

Wesley Yuji Un
115 S. Hamana • Honolulu, Hawaii 96842 • (808) 555-9142

Objective
Position as environmental scientist with an organization involved with the study of oceanic environments and the preservation of the ocean's resources.

Experience
- Developed and maintained the Shell Oil and Hazardous Substance Spill Contingency Plan, effective with all offshore drilling projects in the United States and European countries.
- Developed preparedness training and drills for the corporate crisis management team.
- Researched oil-spill response technologies and ecological effects of oil spills and current cleanup strategies employed by major oil companies.
- Provided scientific information and technical guidance to Shell Oil operating businesses on spill contingency planning.
- Prepared comment and testimony on proposed legislation and regulations at the federal and state levels related to spill prevention and response as well as spill effects on fish, wildlife, and ocean and shore ecology.
- Provided in-house consulting on ecological issues for Shell Oil regional corporate management.
- Led a team to evaluate safety hazards at Shell Oil's offshore refineries following a major spill.
- Coordinated initial companywide implementation of SARA Title III emergency planning and community right-to-know requirements.
- Assisted Shell Oil's Government Affairs Office and the Hawaii Petroleum Council in developing alternative concepts and language for legislation in the Hawaii General Assembly relating to hazardous materials transportation and implementation of SARA Title III requirements in Hawaii.

Employment History
1995 to present	Environmental Regulatory Inspector, United States Environmental Protection Agency, Pacific Islands Region, Honolulu, Hawaii
1991 to 1995	Environmental Scientist, Division of Health, State of Hawaii, Honolulu
1987 to 1991	Manager, Ecology and Contingency Plans; Corporate Health, Safety, and Environmental Quality Department; Shell Oil; San Diego, California

Education
Postgraduate study in hazardous waste issues, University of Hawaii, 1997–1998
M.S. in Environmental Sciences, University of Hawaii, 1994
B.S. in Biology, University of Oregon, 1987

References on request

THOMAS J. HAMMERSKJELD

7715 Weston Park Lane • Charlotte, NC 28214 • Cellular phone: 704-555-2866

REGISTRATION

Registered Environmental Professional
National Registry of Environmental Professionals

EXPERIENCE

Seven years of experience in the environmental engineering field, including managerial and program administration in land development, solid waste, and energy-related projects.

➤ Types of projects: waste-to-energy, fossil fuel and hydroelectric generation, geothermal energy recovery, municipal waste landfills, solid waste resource and energy recovery, and solid waste management planning.

➤ Technical experience: development and preparation of engineering feasibility studies, regulatory licensing documents, siting studies, environmental impact assessments, and environmental permitting.

➤ Managerial experience: developing and implementing project management techniques and tools, establishing project formats and protocols, developing and maintaining client contact, and reporting project progress.

RECENT ACCOMPLISHMENTS

Project manager for the successful completion of a comprehensive and integrated solid waste management project for a central New York State county project.

➤ Developed a comprehensive recycling analysis and recycling plan; a comprehensive solid waste management plan, including a generic environmental impact statement and a landfill siting study. Coordinated permitting of a new countywide landfill, involving the preparation of a detailed hydrogeologic investigation, detailed engineering design, and environmental impact statement to fulfill solid waste management and environmental quality review requirements of the state of North Carolina.

➤ Assisted in the development and production of a project managers' manual for Moore EnviroTech, Inc. Compiled and reviewed technical sections of the document as well as developed and prepared sample work plans and completed forms.

➤ Spoke at two national conferences for two national associations—engineering and environmental—presenting the results of successful siting and permitting projects for solid waste facilities.

TECHNICAL AREAS OF EXPERTISE

Environmental Permitting

➤ Gained working knowledge of numerous regulatory programs at federal and state levels, including FERC, Sub Titles C and D (RCRA), NEPA, NPDES (storm water), CWA—Section 404 (wetlands), and CZM

Environmental Impact Assessment

➤ Conducted numerous environmental assessments and evaluations on projects as small as a 20 TPD solid waste transfer station to a large Midwest nuclear generating facility. Prepared numerous environmental impact statements in several states for both private companies as well as government agencies.

Feasibility Study

➤ Performed both environmental and engineering feasibility studies for potential projects ranging from small sand and gravel mines to large hydroelectric and waste-to-energy facilities. Worked with private companies as well as government agencies, and in a number of states.

Siting Studies

➤ Have conducted siting studies for potential facilities ranging from small, solid waste management facilities to large hydroelectric facilities for private companies, authorities, and governmental agencies.

Communication Skills

➤ Developed good communicative skills, including report writing, proposal preparation, and verbal articulation. Performed technical and editorial review for document consistency and presentation.

EMPLOYMENT HISTORY

1991 - 2002 Moore EnviroTech, Inc., Charlotte, NC
Since 1991, Senior Environmental Scientist

1985 - 1991 Fisher & Parkfield Engineering Corporation, Syracuse, NY
Titled Scientist - Hydrologist

EDUCATION

M.S. - Forestry - Syracuse University (1991)
B.S. - Geology, minor in Hydrology - Barton College (1985)

◆ TALBOT HUNTER

Route 6E, Stop 1156 • Chugiak, Alaska 99623 • (907) 555-3911 • thunter@xxx.com

◆ PROFESSIONAL OBJECTIVE

An engineering management position with a firm specializing in environmental projects.

◆ PROFESSIONAL EXPERIENCE

Director of Technical Services
Al-Can Engineering, Ltd., Anchorage, Alaska, 1997 to present

Supervise technical operations for regional offices in Alaska, British Columbia, and Alberta. Develop design standards, implement project management and project control systems, and supervise construction at project sites. Work with senior technical experts from all divisions, including chief engineer, chief hydrogeologist, chief compliance officer, chief construction manager, and the directors of bioremediation technology and health and safety.

Executive Engineer
Mentor GeoSystems, Inc., Anchorage, Alaska, 1994 to 1997

Prepared environmental impact statement, terrain sensitivity report, and design of river-crossing constructs. Prepared design manual for drainage and erosion control for Yukon Latera Pipeline. Prepared final geotechnical report for submission to the federal government on the design and construction of the trans-Canada natural gas pipeline.

Engineering Specialist
CH2M Hill, Engineering Consultants, Denver, Colorado, 1990 to 1994

Reviewed geologic, hydrologic, geotechnical, and thermal design for trans-Canada natural gas pipeline. Assisted in establishing criteria for environmental protection, erosion control procedures, foundations, slope stability, surface and groundwater hydrology, design of drainage structures, and general civil construction techniques. Conducted detailed review of quality control plans. Provided on-site monitoring and technical assistance. Began employment as intern and was hired full-time upon degree completion.

◆ EDUCATION

B.S., Civil Engineering, cum laude, University of Colorado, Denver, 1990

Founding member of student chapter of the American Society of Civil Engineers; served two years as president. Initiated program for on-site training and student internships with several local engineering firms, in cooperation with the College of Engineering.

Susan G. Griffith

8281 S. Becker Ave.   Anchorage, Alaska 99574   907-555-9223   griffith@xxx.com

Employment Objective

Research Scientist/Project Leader for oceanic mammal research endeavor or consulting project.

Current Position

Sea Otter Research Project Leader
(1999 grant-funded project closes April 2002)
Alaska Fish and Wildlife Research Center, Anchorage

Design and implement sea otter research program in Alaska. Prepare and approve study plans, supervise research projects and prepare results for publication. Management of project staff. Direct funding allocations.

Previous Positions

Wildlife Biologist (GS-486-09), 1997–1999
Koyukuk/Nowitna National Wildlife Refuge Complex
U.S. Fish and Wildlife Service, Galena, Alaska

Fish and Wildlife Biologist (GS-401-07), 1994–1997
National Ecology Research Center, U.S. Fish and Wildlife Service
Santa Cruz Field Station, Santa Cruz, California

Biological Technician (Wildlife: GS-404-05), 1992–1994
National Ecology Research Center, U.S. Fish and Wildlife Service
San Simeon Field Station, San Simeon, California

Education and Training

1997—Arctic Survival Course, U.S. Air Force, Elmendorf AFB, Anchorage, Alaska
1996—Certified Radio Telephone Operator, third class,
    U.S. Department of Commerce
1992—M.S., Wildlife Biology, California Polytechnic State University,
    San Luis Obispo
1990—B.S., Biology, Long Beach State University, Long Beach, California

Society Memberships

Society for Marine Mammalogy
American Society of Mammalogists
The Wildlife Society
Western Society of Naturalists
National Geographic Society

ANWAR B. VEGAZZI
Environmental Scientist

452 W. Magnolia Blvd.
Jackson, MS 39211
(601) 555-2419
vegazzi@xxx.com

Professional Objective

Senior Environmental Scientist position with a public or private agency involved in waste resource recovery technologies that will enable me to bring innovative recovery strategies to profitable use.

Employment History

PROJECT MANAGER
Jackson County Landfill, Jackson County Department of Waste Management
Jackson, MS, 1999

- Prepared comprehensive recycling analysis and solid waste management assessment.
- Wrote solid waste management plan; coordinated approval by regulatory agencies.
- Prepared environmental impact assessment, including study of impact on wetlands, archaeological heritage sites, and groundwater movement.
- Wrote and gained approval for final environmental impact statement.
- Supervised construction and initial operations of site.

MANAGER
Debenhorst Recycling Corp.
Jackson, MS, 1996–1999

- Developed a solid waste permit application package for a construction and demolition landfill.
- Provided detailed hydrogeologic investigation.
- Worked with engineering specialists to develop engineering design.
- Drafted environmental impact statement.
- Worked with marketing specialists to develop program of information regarding recycling services.
- Managed all aspects of corporate development, including personnel hiring and firing, budget management, and capitalization efforts.

Page 1 of 2

TASK MANAGER
Mississippi Resource Recovery Project, Resource Recoveries, Inc.
Jackson, MS, 1993–1996
- Worked on development of a solid waste resource recovery project for the entire state.
- Prepared draft and final environmental impact report for a 1,500 ton-per-day facility in Brandon, Mississippi.
- Prepared similar reports for accompanying residue landfill in nearby Value, Mississippi.
- Worked with hydrologists, geoscientists, and engineers to determine optimum siting for both facilities.
- In a separate project, prepared the delineation and classification of a disturbed wetlands area proposed for development; presented alternative measures not only to protect, but also to enhance wetlands as part of development project that were agreed upon and successfully implemented.

Education and Training

Certification in Environmental Science, 1993
Center for the Study and Preservation of Environmental Resources, Chicago, IL

Bachelor of Science degrees in Geology and Engineering Technology, 1992
Stevens Institute of Technology, Hoboken, NJ

Research Associate, Professor Michael J. Reynolds, 1990–1992
Stevens Institute of Technology, Hoboken, NJ
On-the-job training in environmental engineering technology.

Memberships and Affiliations

International Geological Union
Institute of Environmental Sciences and Technology
Union of Concerned Scientists
The Nature Conservancy

References available on request.

Dorian G. Bixby

P.O. Box 341   Bar Harbor, Maine 04690   207-555-4493

Education
Colorado State University, Fort Collins
1990 - Master of Science
Major: Animal Sciences, Animal Breeding, Genetics
Thesis: Effect of diet and age on reproduction in obese and lean mice.

South Dakota State University, Brookings
1988 - Bachelor of Science
Major: Animal Sciences
Minors: Genetics, Statistics

Professional Experience
**Currently, self-employed as a consultant after having relocated to Bar
Harbor, Maine, March 2000 to present**
Clients: U.S. Fish and Wildlife Service, National Research Council, Marine
Mammals Research Center, University of Maine.

**Biologist, Alaska Fish and Wildlife Research Center, Anchorage
November 1995 to March 2000**
Researched marbled murrelets, with emphasis on studies of acute and
chronic effects of the Exxon Valdez oil spill on the birds.

**Staff Associate, National Research Council Board on Agriculture,
Washington, Pennsylvania, March 1990 to November 1995**
Worked with the Committee on Managing Global Genetic Resources on a
series of reports assessing the status of and need to conserve genetic diversity in economically important species.

**Graduate Research Assistant, Department of Animal Sciences,
September 1988 to March 1990**
Colorado State University, Fort Collins
Performed statistical analyses of data. Assisted in teaching several under-
graduate courses.

Research and Professional Interests
Mammalian genetics and physiology
Quantitative genetics
Management of genetic diversity in animal and bird populations
Reproduction of endangered species

References and complete c.v. available upon request.

Benson Wiley Jr.

33 Fenton Creek Road
Charleston, West Virginia 25309
(304) 555-2268

Employment Objective

Obtain Research Associate position with an academic or private research organization involved in studies of toxic substances in air and water and their impact on bird and mammal survival and reproduction rates.

Education

M.S., Animal Science and Genetics

University of British Columbia, Vancouver
Degree awarded 2000, with distinction

> Thesis: The relationship between male fertility and nuclear chromatin structure of spermatozoa from mammalian species, including bulls, rams, stallions, rats, and humans.

B.S., Wildlife Biology

West Virginia University, Morgantown
Degree awarded 1995, with honors

> Honors Project: Decline in coyote population in Appalachian Mountains, 1991–1995, with bibliography of historic surveys of coyote population.

Experience

Research Assistant, Department of Animal Sciences
University of British Columbia, 1996–2000

> Taught undergraduate courses in Animal Science and Biochemistry. Conducted research on population genetics of great horned owls in wild versus in captivity.

Assistant, Biochemistry Laboratory, West Virginia University
College of Science, 1993–1994

> Assisted in ongoing studies utilizing flow cytometry to evaluate toxic effects on male reproductive function.

Memberships

National Mammal Research Council
National Audubon Society
American Genetics Association

References and transcripts available on request.

Katherine Milton

Route 5, Box 26E   Home: 406-555-4493
Great Falls, Montana 59411   E-mail: K.E.Milton@xxx.com

EDUCATION
Bachelor of Science degree, Wildlife Biology
University of Wisconsin, Madison - 1999

FIELD SKILLS
Radio telemetry (fixed-wing aircraft, boat, land). Capture and handling of: birds of prey, ornate box turtles, mule deer, pronghorn antelope, and small mammals. Water and vegetation sampling. Horsemanship safety certification (1990). Four-wheel-drive operation and maintenance. Freshwater and marine boat mainte-nance. Canoeing skills. Tree- and rock-climbing skills. Field use of topographic maps, compass, pH and conductivity meters, light meter, soil corer, tree corer, posthole driver, chain saw, skill and table saws, drill press, and power drill.

TECHNICAL SKILLS
Parametric statistics. Computers (D-base, SAS, Turbo, Lotus 1-2-3, Pascal pro-gramming). Word processing (Corel WordPerfect, WordStar). Drafting figures for publication. Water chemistry. Blood analysis. Scientific writing (quarterly and final reports). Library research.

PUBLICATION
Milton, Katherine, and J. F. Simon. The demography and ecology of the ornate box turtle (*Terrapene omata*) in south-central Wisconsin. *Wildlife Biologist* 6, no. 3: 93–104.

EMPLOYMENT
July 1999 - present
Technical Assistant, Department of Natural Resources, Great Falls, Montana
- Conduct aerial and ground surveys to locate and monitor raptor nests, includ-ing collection and identification of nest prey remains, banding, weighing, and age estimation of young.
- Implement habitat enhancement, including placement of perch poles and nest-ing platforms.
- Monitor small mammal populations on enhancement areas to determine effects of increased water availability.
- Write quarterly and annual reports.
- Supervise two field assistants and one lab assistant.

Personal and professional references available upon request.

FARAH L. YSAMI

554 Longview Street
Littleton, Colorado 80104
303-555-9334

EDUCATION

Bachelor of Science in Biology with a minor in Wildlife Biology, 1998, University of Minnesota, Minneapolis

EXPERIENCE

June 1998 to present
Assistant Biologist
Fish and Game Commission of Colorado, Littleton
Responsibilities
- Monitor flyway Canada goose harvest for agricultural and sport permits.
- Respond to public inquiries regarding Colorado's wildlife management programs.
- Monitor radio-transmitted responses from tagged birds and animals.
- Enter data into database files and collate data.
- Test experimental capture techniques.
- Analyze vegetation/food supply as part of fieldwork.
- Write monthly and quarterly reports to submit to federal agency.
- Assist with annual counts of wildlife population in western and central regions of Colorado.

Required Knowledge
- Colorado's waterfowl hunting regulations.
- Population biology of the flyway.
- Colorado wildlife management plan and population surveys.

Camp Counselor, summers 1995 to 1997
Anagama Canoe Camp, Littleton, Colorado
Responsibilities
- Taught informational sessions on the local ecology.
- Taught canoeing and canoe safety classes.
- Guided 30- to 70-mile canoe trips with groups of 8 to 10 campers, ages 12 to 18.
- Served as camp cook while at base camp.

Required Knowledge
- Certification in wilderness survival lifesaving and CPR.
- Full understanding of local ecology and topography.

REFERENCES

Available upon request.

• Dana M. Parker •
Route 3, Box 195
Twin Falls, Idaho 83302

• • •

• Professional Objective

Field biologist in the area of fisheries and wildlife. Especially interested in working with impact of changes in logging management on populations of native species.

• Experience

Laboratory Technician
University of Idaho, Department of Biology
October 2000 to June 2002
- Entered and edited large data sets.
- Ran basic statistical analyses.
- Gained full operating knowledge of DOS 3.1, SAS, Cyber Systems, IBM.
- Created biological illustrations and drafted figures for publication.
- Wrote, edited, and conducted library research.

Student Intern
Idaho Department of Fish and Wildlife
Summer 1999
- Obtained baseline data on water chemistry and vegetation sampling.
- Assisted with fisheries population studies.
- Established field counting procedures.
- Prepared final project report.

Laboratory Assistant
University of Idaho, Department of Biology
September 1998 to June 2000 (excluding summer 1999)
- Curated university mammalogy collection.
- Prepared carcass and study skins for the museum collection.
- Prepared student general biology labs.

• Education

B.S., Fisheries and Wildlife Biology - University of Idaho, 2001

References and transcripts provided on request.

Bradford Powers

4432 S. Kirkview Street
Olympia, Washington 98221
(206) 555-2284

Objective

Research scientist position on a project involving population studies for species on or in consideration for the endangered list.

Educational Background

M.S. in Wildlife Biology - anticipated March 2002
University of Washington, Seattle
Thesis: Productivity and Dynamics in Rainforest Ecosystems: Olympic National Wildlife Refuge, Olympic Peninsula

B.S. in Wildlife Biology - June 1998 - University of Washington, Seattle

Additional Research Projects

University of Washington - Ecology and Behavioral Biology, 2000
Received a grant from The Wildlife Society to conduct a pilot study that examined the mechanism of a universal self-thinning rule (Yoda, 1963), based on the mathematical relationship observed between plant-stand density and aboveground biomass as density increases. The final report provided the necessary information for additional grants to continue work in this area.

Piñon Canyon Maneuver Site - Summer Internship
U.S. Fish and Wildlife Service, 1998
Participated in the capture and tagging of adult pronghorn antelope, aerial line transect and quadrat surveys for mule deer, and net-gun recapture of adult mule deer to replace inactive radio collars.

Personal Qualifications

Interact well with members of a crew as well as private land owners, special interest groups, and the general public as a result of cooperative work with various field teams and agencies. Master's thesis project involved both field and laboratory work, as well as statistical analyses on gathered data sets.

Professional Memberships

The Wildlife Society
The Nature Conservancy

TIMOTHY B. HANSON
211 Red Bridge Road
International Falls, Minnesota 56649
218-555-2238

EDUCATION
Patterson College, Duluth, Minnesota, 1994–1998
Bachelor of Science in Biology, 1998

PROFESSIONAL EXPERIENCE
Biological Technician, July 1998–present
Minnesota Fish and Wildlife Research Station, International Falls
Collected and analyzed field data for Freshwater Cutthroat Trout Project.
Supervisor: Jane Albright

Lab Animal Technician, September 1997–June 1998
Patterson College, Department of Biochemistry
Collected data from and maintained captive wolf colony.
Supervisor: Dr. Anne Steel

Wildlife Technician (Intern), June–September 1997
U.S. Fish and Wildlife Service, Kawishiwi Field Laboratory, St. Paul,
Minnesota
Collected field data for Wolf/Deer Project
Supervisor: Dr. Mitchell Finley

Veterinary Assistant (Volunteer), June–September 1995 and 1996
Spielsand Animal Hospital, International Falls, Minnesota
Assisted in small animal treatments and served as night emergency attendant.
Supervisor: Dr. John Spielsand

Ranch Hand, June–September 1994
Double D Bar J Ranch, Butte, Montana
Assisted in Quarter Horse Breeding Program.
Supervisor: Dave Bellows

AWARDS
Exceptional Merit Award for a Student Intern, U.S. Fish and Wildlife Service,
1997

Special Achievement Award, Patterson College, 1994

Gregory M. Sherman

3341 Terra Lane, No. 54 • Denver, Colorado 80231 • 303/555-2248

Education	Graduate Study, Range and Wildlife Management Utah State University, 1988 Bachelors Degree, Forestry (Wildlife/Zoology Minor) Pennsylvania State University, 1986
Work Experience	**Forestry/Agro-Forestry Consultant to the Government of Kenya** **Under Contract with Texas A&M University and USAID** **June 2000 to December 2002** • Served as a technician/consultant to the government of Kenya in the areas of range, ranch, and livestock development, planning, and programming. Trained Kenyan ranch managers and directors. Developed ranch and range management curricula at Egerton College and University of Nairobi while a PASA with USAID. Spent 2001 as a technical consultant/contractor with Texas A&M University staff, conducting a forestry, agro-forestry preinvestment study of Laikipia District in northern Kenya as a member of a multidisciplinary team of Americans, British, and Kenyans. **Ranger/Assistant Supervisor on Western Forests** **International Forestry Staff, Washington, DC, and other locations** **June 1986 to June 2000 (with leave for graduate study in 1988)** • Assumed responsibility for management, planning, programming, and obtained field experience in timber and fuelwood management (reforestation, thinning, pruning, nursery development, ponderosa pine bark beetle control, fire control, range management), as well as wildlife and watershed management. Worked on four western national forest districts (average size 300,000 acres). Promoted to assistant supervisor in 1989.
Recognition	• Outstanding Forest Service Middle Management Trainee, 1985 • Assigned as personal assistant to the USAID representative to the United Nations • Selected for special international assignments as USFS representative
Language Skills	Speaking ability in both Swahili and French; limited written French
Other Skills	Video and still photography, especially for purposes of documentation
References	Available upon request

Hampton Avery III

175 SE River View Road   Arcata, California 95522
707-555-4433   E-mail: Hampton.avery@xxx.com

PROFESSIONAL GOAL
Range and resource management position

EDUCATION
M.S., Rangeland Management, University of Wyoming, Laramie, 2000
B.S., Forestry, Humboldt State University, Arcata, California, 1998

EXPERIENCE
June 1998 to present
Forester, Wyoming Department of Forestry, Laramie
Responsibilities:
- Monitor damage from grazing of wildlife and livestock.
- Assist with field studies of impact of livestock grazing on regrowth of forest.
- Assist with counts to estimate yield for timber sales.
- Monitor compliance with rangeland management plan.
- Master federal and state legislation regarding rangeland resource management.

June 1999 to September 1999
Forestry Intern, California Department of Forestry, Arcata
Responsibilities:
- Maintained public facilities in Redwoods National Forest.
- Assisted forest rangers with routine field checks.
- Provided information assistance in the District Office.
- Prepared text and graphs for publication on rangeland management in Redwoods National Forest.

AWARDS
Best Graduate Project Award, University of Wyoming, 2000
Dean's List, Humboldt State University, 1997, 1998
Morrison Scholarship for Forestry Conservation Study, 1995, 1997, 1998, 1999

References provided on request.

T R E V O R   G A I N E S

Route 6, Box 142
Galveston, Texas 77552
409/555-3341

PROFESSIONAL OBJECTIVE

■ Ornithological Research Scientist for an organization interested in the study of birds of prey.

EXPERIENCE AND QUALIFICATIONS

■ Pursue interest in ornithology through self-teaching; strong educational background in zoology and entomology.

■ Assist with annual Audubon counts of shorebirds in Gulf Coast region.

■ Wrote informational booklet, "Identifying the Birds of Southeast Texas," published by the Audubon Society, Galveston, Texas.

■ Completed grant-funded research project on the habitat and reproduction of peregrine falcons on the Edwards Plateau.

■ Studied eagle habitat in western British Columbia as part of a multinational survey funded by the National Audubon Societies of Canada and the United States.

■ Worked as a field scientist on a project studying the diet of Gulf Coast shorebirds and the impact of toxins on life span and reproduction.

■ Handled and treated injured raptors while volunteering at the Raptor Rehabilitation Hospital in Beaumont, Texas.

WORK HISTORY

■ Consultant, Audubon Society, Galveston, Texas, 2000 to present
■ Technician, Galveston Research Station, Texas Division of Wildlife Management, Galveston, 1996 to 2000

EDUCATION

B.S., Zoology and Entomology (dual major), University of North Texas, Denton, 1996

Publication list and references provided on request.

Tamara S. McDonald

Permanent Address:
2665 Pleasantville Valley Road
Winnemucca, Nevada 89445
(702) 555-4493 (messages only)

Current Address:
P.O. Box 3412
Moscow, Idaho 83843
(208) 555-2295

Objective
Entry-level position with an organization focused on natural resource management.

Experience
Student Intern, Idaho Department of Conservation,
Division of Land Management, Moscow, Idaho, Research Station,
March to August 2001

> Worked full-time for six months (three months on an internship basis and three as a contract employee, hired upon successful completion of internship). Assisted the field biologist in the Division of Wildlife in areas such as natural heritage, forest resources, fisheries, habitat manipulation, and research. Received formal training through seminars and workshops. Also assisted with environmental education programming, identified and researched natural vegetation and wildlife, and cataloged natural formations and historic landmarks.

Instructor, Outdoor School Instruction Program, Cheney School District, Cheney, Washington, spring 1995, 1997, 1998

> Served as team leader in developing environmental education program for students in grades 5 and 6. Taught 3 one-week sessions at Cheney Outdoor School.

Education
Bachelor of Science degree, Natural Sciences, December 2001
University of Idaho, Moscow

Leadership Experience
Vice President, Natural Sciences Student Coalition, 1999

Team Leader, Outdoor School Instruction Program, Cheney School District, 1995 to 1998

References and college transcripts available upon request.

RUBY J. SANDERS
P.O. Box 58 • Wells, NV 89835 • (702) 555-3357

OBJECTIVE
An internship with an organization involved with resource management or conservation.

EDUCATION
Currently working toward bachelor of science degree in Minerals Engineering at the Colorado School of Mines, Golden, CO. Anticipated completion date, June 2002.

Courses:
Mining Technology
Metallurgical Engineering
Mining Engineering
Hydrology
Instrumentation
Computational Fluid Dynamics
Environmental Engineering
Mining Waste Treatment
Chemical Structures Engineering

EXPERIENCE
Minerals Management Volunteer, Rocky Mountain National Forest, Central District
Mountain City, CO
July - September 2001

Responsibilities: Assisted forester in inspecting mining activities.
Monitored reclamation and aspen regeneration studies.
Helped with recreation projects and administration.
Performed minor maintenance duties.
Participated in groundwater studies.

Assistant Night Manager, Dale's In and Out Drive-in
Wells, NV
September 1998 to present

Responsibilities: Provide customer service and monitor sales.
Tally cash accurately and write inventory reports.
Assume responsibility for sole management of swing shift for small 24-hour restaurant.
Manage personnel and determine scheduling.
Oversee all aspects of small restaurant operation.

References on request

SHERICE BUGNI

Route 2, Box 55-1
Roanoke, Virginia 24002
703-555-1288

OBJECTIVE
A position in environmental education and recreation with a parks, forest, or conservation organization or agency.

EDUCATION
B.S.—Environmental Science/Resource Management, March 2000
Jefferson State College, Roanoke, Virginia
Concentrations: Ecology, Biogeology, Cultural Resources, and Natural Resources

EXPERIENCE
Volunteer/Environmental Education Intern
Summers—1996 to present
Jefferson Forest Preserves, Roanoke, Virginia
Teach classes in ecology, cultural resources, botany, bird identification, wildlife tracking, and forest management. Work with the general public by leading guided forest tours. Raise awareness and appreciation of nature and increase understanding of environmental issues.

Volunteer/Interpreter
Summer 1995
Virginia Museum of Science and Industry, Roanoke, Virginia
Worked with elementary school children on special projects with the museum's education staff, including segments on dinosaurs, geology, botany, chemistry, and biology. Helped to coordinate student assistant volunteers. Worked part-time (paid) as an interpreter, providing general information to the public on a touring exhibit of extinct and endangered species.

OTHER SKILLS
Excellent written and oral communications skills and management skills. Ability to work effectively with young children and the general public. Computer knowledge for database management, word processing, and some graphic communications programs.

References available on request.

TANI WELCH

231 Grant Avenue • St. Louis, Missouri 63125
314/555-2296 • tani.welch@xxx.com

OBJECTIVE

A position as a bioecologist or natural scientist.

EDUCATION

B.S., Environmental Science
University of Missouri, St. Louis
Expected degree completion date: June 2002

Special Areas of Concentration:

Bioecology

Ecological concepts and processes are applied to coniferous and deciduous forests, deserts, sand dunes, streams, and rivers in field-oriented study. Scientific work experience at field research laboratory looks at mechanisms of plant responses to environmental change caused by humans, including atmospheric, nutrient, water, and global climate factors.

Physical Science

Comprehensive synthesis of the physical sciences explains major processes of the universe, including those of the atmosphere, hydrosphere, geosphere, solar system, and heavens. Advanced work involves a detailed conceptual study of the transformation of thought occasioned by modern physics. Concepts range from classical electricity, magnetism, and light to problems stemming from late 19th-century observations and their comprehension by 20th-century quantum and relativity theories.

Numerical Methods in Environmental Science

Environmental and ecological sciences use modeling and multivariate tools available for research, including hands-on application with real data sets and interpretation of results. Analysis of environmental issues includes data acquisition, synthesis, evaluation, and communication of results.

Environmental Problem Solving

Extensive research and study determines the origins of current environmental problems, primarily related to toxic chemicals in the environment. Investigation reveals current scientific means of analyzing and addressing environmental issues.

WORK HISTORY

Lab Assistant, Plant Pathology Lab, University of Missouri, 2001 to present

Thomas K. Lewis

Route 3, Box 112-5
Big Timber, Montana 59011
(406) 555-4730
tlewis@xxx.com

Career Opportunity Sought

Entry-level position in forest land-management and operations, with specific interest in watershed and soil stabilization management

Educational Background

Forest Engineering, Bachelor of Science degree, 2001
Humboldt State University, Arcata, California

Curriculum

Full complement of Mathematics,
    Biochemistry, and Physics courses
Advanced Forest Surveying
Forest Engineering Computations
Tree Identification
Wood Technology
Engineering: Statics,
    Strength of Materials
Forest Biology
Forest Mensuration
Engineering Properties of Forest Soils
Forest Soil Mechanics

Operations Analysis
Watershed Processes and
    Management Technology
Forest Engineering: Fluid
    Mechanics and Hydrology
Reforestation
Physical Geology for Engineers
Production Planning and Management
Forest Resource Economics and
    Forest Policy
Amenity Resource Management
Principles of Silviculture

Employment Experience

Volunteer Surveyor, U.S. Forest Service, Humboldt National Forest
Part of Student Activism Program, Humboldt State University, summers 1997 to 2000

Memberships

Xi Sigma Pi, national forestry honor society
National Society of Forest Engineers, Student Chapter

References

Available on request

Carey T. Yiu

227 Benson Street SW • Lewiston, Idaho 83502 • 208-555-9122

Job Desired

Entry-level position in Forest Resources Management or Water Resources Management

Education

B.S. in Forestry / Water Resources Management
University of Idaho / 2001

Experience

Research Assistant to Dr. Jane Howard, Professor of Forestry, University of Idaho
1999 to 2001

Areas of Specialization

➤ Watershed Processes / Effects of land-use practices on the physical hydrology (interception, infiltration, evapotranspiration, subsurface flow and surface runoff, water yields, and peak flows) of forested watersheds. Surface erosion, mass soil movements, stream temperatures, nutrient levels, and effects of management activities upon riparian systems. Familiar with U.S. Forest Practice Rules.

➤ Forest Soil Mechanics / Principles of engineering mechanics as applied to soil problems such as slope stability, lateral earth pressure theory, earth retaining structures, and erosion.

➤ Forest Regeneration and Stand Management / Current forest biology information as related to enhancing silviculturist's ability to gather and integrate information on forest sites, to establish alternatives for site manipulation, and to select the approach best suited for proper management of the site.

➤ Natural Resource Planning / Research project development and analysis. Investigative procedures, the principles and ethics of natural resource science, and principles and practices in scientific communication. Hands-on experience in statistical analysis and data management. Experience with widely used commercial statistical software package, SAS, for practical application and actual implementation of statistical analysis techniques.

➤ Forest Ecosystem and Ecology / Dynamics of undisturbed forest ecosystems, responses of ecosystems to perturbation, optimization of response for attainment of management objectives. The structure and function of forests and associated streams in natural and managed ecosystems. Nutrient cycling processes and their long-term effects on forest growth and yield. Current research and growth simulation models.

References

Available on request

CHINA RADES

4409 Westbrook Lane
Rumford, Maine 04277
207-555-2881

OBJECTIVE
Environmental education position involving environmental or cultural resource interpretation.

EDUCATION
University of Maine
B.A., Forestry, 2002
- Degree Options: Cultural Resource Management and Environmental Resource Interpretation
- GPA 3.6; Honors College graduate; Forestry Honor Society

SPECIAL TRAINING
Cultural Resource Management Option
- Anthropology Topics: People of North America; Archaeology of the Northeast; Archaeology Field School; Contemporary Native Americans; Principles of Museum Work
- History Topics: History of American Indians; Historiography; History of American Immigration; Early Settlements of the Northeast; Field Study of Heritage Sites
- Resource Management Topics: Cultural Resource Planning and Management; Cultural Aspects of Recreation; Issues in Resource Management

Environmental Resource Interpretation Option
- Natural History Topics: Contemporary Geology; Geology of the Northeast; Botany; Atmospheric Science; Wildlife Resources; Insect and Vertebrate Biology; Herpetology; Population Dynamics
- Resource Economics Topics: Environmental Economics; Land and Water Economics; Natural Resources Policy; Public Expenditures; Forest Resource Economics
- Forest Resources Topics: Environmental Interpretation; Ecological Aspects of Forest Management; Wilderness Management; Amenity Resource Management; Forest Management Issues.

EXPERIENCE
Assistant Parks Ranger, Maine Department of Parks and Recreation, Rumford
Summers since 1998
- Provide assistance and information to park visitors.
- Work with park rangers on special assignments.
- Assist with maintenance of park facilities.
- Work with school groups visiting the park.
- Lead weekly nature walks.
- Monitor reports of park usage.

Hannah G. Mgana

116 South Frasier Avenue
Mattawan, Michigan 49071
616/555-2290

Education
B.S., Forest Recreation Resource Management, 2002
Syracuse University, Syracuse, New York

Academic Experience
- Recreation Behavior: Principles of human behavior and analysis of recreation management issues. Sociological and psychological approaches to recreation management.
- Recreation Resource Management: Techniques for collection, storage, analysis, and display of recreation resource planning data. Practice in use of recreation planning models. Computer and statistical methods for recreation planning, management, and economic evaluation. Land and water resources used for outdoor recreation. Planning and management of natural and cultural resources for long-term resource productivity, with a focus on rural and wildland areas of forest, range, and lakes.
- Forest Resource Planning and Decision Making: Biological, economic, and amenity characteristics of the forest system in resource management planning and decision making. Practical application of methods in consultation with practitioners.
- Tourism and Outdoor Recreation Issues: Economics of recreation resources. Role of cultural resources in outdoor recreation systems. U.S. historic preservation movement. Legal basis for compliance procedures for federal land-managing agencies. Application of economic concepts to forest recreation management. Tourism planning, management, and environmental impacts.
- Environmental Education: Environmental interpretation of natural and cultural features in parks, museums, and similar settings. Applying effective communication techniques in the development of brochures, exhibits, talks, slide presentations, and tours.

Work History
Student Intern, Backwater Adventures, Inc., Grayling, Michigan, Summer 2000
- Worked with river crews on 8- to 10-day backwater excursions in canoes and kayaks. Served as camp cook. Assisted with packing to assure watertight, secure equipment and supplies. Provided local history, geography, geology, and cultural information for interested participants. Researched local history to prepare informative report used by guides on river tours.

References
Available on request, along with official college transcripts.

DEBORAH SUMMERS

226 West Cray Drive
Martinez, California 94552
510-555-2203

OBJECTIVE

A position in range management, with emphasis on working toward careful conservation of resources, managed for multiple uses.

EDUCATION

Rangeland Resource Management, Bachelor of Science degree
University of California, Santa Cruz, 2002

PROGRAM AREAS OF CONCENTRATION

Rangeland Resources: Integrated land use with emphasis on plant-animal-soil interactions. Use of measurements in resource management. Field practice in wildland and vegetation inventory methods. Potential rangeland management problems—regionally, nationally, and internationally. Administration and management of rangelands; planning processes involving goal setting, inventories, personnel management, environment, conflict resolution, and other constraints necessary for effective decision making. Worked with team to analyze data collected from field problems to create plan for local rangeland conflicts.

Desert Watershed Management: Managing rangeland for optimum production and regulation of water yields, as well as maintaining soil stability and on-site productivity. Effects of grazing herbivores and their potential as land-use, manipulative tools. Concepts of arid land hydrology, with emphasis on the resultant effects on runoff quantity and quality.

Grassland and Arid Ecosystems: Extensive study of species occurring in arid land biomes of the United States, including both scientific and common names, ecological requirements and tolerances, reaction to grazing, and their value as forage and cover. Emphasis on North American grasslands, with study of system structure, process, and function as well as phytoedaphic and zootic relationships.

EXPERIENCE

Student Intern: Director of Range Management, Sonoma County, California
Summer 1998

RESPONSIBILITIES

Assisted with the development of ecological monitoring procedures for ranches operating in Sonoma County. Worked with ecological monitoring teams on two rangeland management sites. Participated in training program for ecological monitoring teams.

References will be provided upon request.

Jason Varley Jr.

2119-A Sperry Road   **(216) 555-2294**
Mentor, Ohio 44060   **j.varley@xxx.com**

Objective   Seeking a position in wildlife biology, preferably on a wildlife refuge or bird sanctuary.

Experience   **Student Intern, summers 1999 and 2000**
Hawk Mountain Sanctuary
RD 2, Hawk Mountain Road
Kempton, Pennsylvania 19529
1999: Served as management intern and learned sanctuary management through training and hands-on experience in education, fund-raising, research, and maintenance. Involved in outdoor education/environmental education pertaining to raptor conservation and the northern Appalachian ecosystem. **2000:** Taught daily courses to organized school groups and the visiting public. Served as research intern and assisted with the design and implementation of research projects and ongoing projects.

Education   **Bachelor of Science, Wildlife Resources/Forestry, 2000**
Ohio University, Zanesville

Courses of Study:
Principles of Wildlife Conservation
Wildlife Resources: Mammals
Wildlife Resources: Birds
Population Dynamics
General Ecology
Ecological Methods
Biology of Game Birds
Management of Big Game Animals
Natural Resource Communication
Recreation Resource Management
Environmental Interpretation

Awards   2000 Student of the Year Award, College of Forestry, Ohio University
1999 Academic Achievement Award, Ohio University
1998 Michelson Scholarship, Ohio University

References   Provided on request.

MARK SPERRY
14 West Hunter Drive • Bend, Oregon 97701
Cellular: (503) 555-1299 • Home: (503) 555-8863

OBJECTIVE
A position as a consultant with an organization dedicated to the conservation of public lands for the wise use and management of our natural resources.

EXPERIENCE
Range, Wildlife, Watershed Management Staff Officer
Forest Information Training and Safety Officer
Deschutes National Forest, Bend, Oregon
September 1991 to present
- Supervise, plan, and develop resource plans and programs for both forest management and safety as principal assistant to the Forest Supervisor.
- Supervise range ecological monitoring program.
- Carry out range and livestock inspections on 42 allotments.
- Coordinate management of over one million acres of rangelands with 70 to 100 forest permits under my supervision.
- Coordinate range, wildlife, and watershed programs with the U.S. Bureau of Reclamation, U.S. Bureau of Indian Affairs, Warm Spring Native American tribe, U.S. Fish and Wildlife Service, and Oregon Wildlife Commission.
- Planned and coordinated the Forest Wildlife Improvement Program with the Oregon Wildlife Commission. Jointly implemented the program.
- Participated in developing an integrated land-use plan for the Deschutes National Forest.
- Organized and established the first Osprey Management Unit on the National Forest. Program deemed a success within four years.

District Ranger, Snow Mountain District
Ochoco National Forest, Burns, Oregon
September 1987 to September 1991
- Developed ecological monitoring programs for all rangeland allotments.
- Developed management plans for all aspects of land use.
- Managed timber sale program.
- Managed reforestation and timber stand improvement program.
- Maintained fire control crews that incorporated public and private resources.
- Developed and implemented an erosion control plan.

EDUCATION
B.S. in Forestry Resource Management, August 1986
Oregon State University, Corvallis, Oregon

Carol Sutter

RR 2, Box 1276
Waterbury Center, VT 05677
802-555-1002
Carol.Sutter@xxx.com

Career Desired	*Recreation management position involved with encouraging outdoor recreation that incorporates environmental education and preservation.*
Education	**2001, B.S. degree in Recreation Management University of Vermont, Burlington**

Program of Study
- ❖ Recreation Field Experience
- ❖ Mapping and Topography
- ❖ Ecological Aspects of Park Management
- ❖ Historical and Cultural Aspects of Recreation
- ❖ Interpretive Education: Cultural Resources
- ❖ Interpretive Education: Environmental Resources
- ❖ Recreational Resource Management
- ❖ Recreational Behavior and Management
- ❖ Natural Resource Communication
- ❖ Recreation Resource Planning

Experience

Intern, Green Mountain Club, summer 2001 Waterbury Center, VT

Responsibilities
Built bridges and brush trails.
- ❖ Performed light construction and drainage work.
- ❖ Maintained shelters.
- ❖ Interacted with the public.
- ❖ Provided information on mountain ecology and mountain safety.

Memberships

Pi Kappa Phi National Honor Society
University of Vermont Rock Climbing Club

References available on request.

KITTY SUVER

223 Becker Road, SW   Cheyenne, Wyoming 82002
(307) 555-0993   kitty.suver@xxx.com

GOAL
Public relations/marketing representative and ecotour provider for firm involved in ecotourism.

EXPERIENCE
TOUR GUIDE, FOSSIL RIM WILDLIFE CENTER
GLEN ROSE, TEXAS—SUMMER 2002
> Led groups of 12 to 14 individuals, ages 8 to 74, on horseback along 43-mile tour of wildlife refuge. Trained to provide information on wildlife, ecology, cultural history, and preservation programs at the center.

WHITEWATER GUIDE, YELLOWSTONE RIVER ADVENTURES
CANYON, WYOMING—SUMMERS 2000 AND 2001
> Served as one of three guides per tour on four- and five-day whitewater trips on the Yellowstone River. Provided information about all aspects of river lore, history, geography, geology, and ecology.

HORSE TRAINER, RIVER RIM RANCH
CANYON, WYOMING—SUMMER 1999
> Worked with young, untrained horses to begin training for trail riding. Assisted in providing riding lessons. Led some trail rides.

EDUCATION
BACHELOR'S DEGREE, PUBLIC RELATIONS MANAGEMENT/TOURISM, 2001
UNIVERSITY OF WYOMING
MINOR IN ENVIRONMENTAL ECOLOGY STUDIES
> Relevant areas of study: Environmental and ecological interpretation and education; understanding theories and planning processes of tourism and tourism management; marketing for tourism and travel; integrating economic, political, social, and cultural impacts on tourism.

MEMBERSHIPS
American Hiking Society
The International Ecotourism Society

REFERENCES
Provided on request. Transcripts also available.

Brandon Naylor
5334 West Elmwood
Seattle, Washington 98002
(206) 555-2093

Professional Objective
Assistant to the director or consultant in the area of environmental health safety.

Educational Background
Bachelor's degree in Environmental Health Safety, 2000
University of Toronto, Ontario, Canada

Areas of Academic Concentration
Environmental Health: Environmental factors affecting public health; epidemiologic approach for assessing biological and chemical exposure and the occurrence of disease; infectious agents and chemicals in the environment; ionizing radiation; protection of the air and water environment; occupational health; solid and hazardous waste management. Magnitude of solid and hazardous waste problem; assessing the environmental impact of waste disposal; methods for detecting adverse health impacts.

Environmental Epidemiology and Public Policy: Application of epidemiologic methodology to environmental health problems; etiologic research in studying traditional environmental health issues related to air, soil, and water pollution, environmental diseases such as cancer and exposures such as pesticides and occupational toxins; policy related to environmental disease control.

Environmental Safety Assurance: Strategies and tactics for recognizing, evaluating, and controlling environmental hazards and hazardous exposures. Application methods designed to optimize safety-related performance. Disaster and security preparedness.

Experience
Research Assistant, Dr. Marvel Cone, University of Toronto, 1998 - 2000
Assisted with epidemiologic research project on the environmental health impact of a toxic waste facility.

References and transcripts provided on request.

SUSAN B. JENNER   77 SW First Street, Apt. 12
Tacoma Park, MD 20912
301-555-3448

OBJECTIVE   Internship in the field of environmental public policy.

EDUCATION   **Environmental Science**
University of Maryland, College Park
1998 to present
Anticipated graduation date, June 2002

Courses completed toward bachelor's degree:
• Organic Chemistry
• Biochemistry
• Human Impacts on Ecosystems
• Environmental Problem Solving
• Analysis of Environmental Issues
• Environmental Interpretation
• American Constitutional Law
• American Environmental Policy
• Photojournalism
• Cultural Resources Management
• Public Administration
• Bureau Politics and the Policy Process
• The Politics of Environmental Problems
• The Public Economy
• Political Analysis and Public Opinion

WORK HISTORY   Office Assistant, College of Science
University of Maryland, College Park
September 1999 to present

Waitress, Joey's Place
Tacoma Park, MD
June 1998 to September 1999

REFERENCES   Available on request.

Kevin Wassai
P.O. Box 652 • Cedar City, Utah 84720 • 801-555-3911

Job Goal
Administrative assistant with organization involved with environmental resource issues.

Experience
Student Intern, May-September 2001
Environmental Action, Inc.
Washington, DC
Supervisor: Mary Beth Harty

Served as administrative/development intern. Maintained contribution records and assisted with fund-raising and development strategies. Conducted research in grant fund-raising. Coordinated administrative operations, organized documents, and participated in outreach to the general public. Assisted magazine interns with editing news stories and providing ideas for future news articles. Maintained in-house information sheet on new public policy decisions affecting pesticide use, toxic and hazardous waste, and general environmental issues.

Education
Bachelor of Science degree, anticipated March 2002
Business Administration with minor in Public Policy
Brigham Young University, Provo, Utah

Awards
Outstanding Service Merit Award, Environmental Action, Inc.
Grayson Scholarship for an Outstanding Business Senior
Dean's List

Memberships
Student Council for Environmental Action
Utah Student Public Interest Group
Business Students Union
Brigham Young University Student Council, Senator for Business

JARRED W. CONLIFF

4644 Southwest Marine Drive • Stoneybrook, California 94311
(810) 555-3488 • E-mail: jarred.conliff@xxx.com

OBJECTIVE
A position in environmental engineering with responsibility for facilities management.

QUALIFICATIONS SUMMARY
Petrophysical engineer with strengths in treatment and disposal of hazardous and toxic waste, analyzing natural and occupational environments for pollution, managing waste remediation, planning disposal and treatment of hazardous waste, designing and operating air and water pollution control equipment, and administering waste management systems.

PROFESSIONAL EXPERIENCE
General Field Engineer, California-Pacific Power Company, 1997 to present
La Jolla, California
- Managed hazardous waste remediation program for nuclear wastewater from four facilities.
- Designed water pollution control units for relay stations.
- Earned three promotions in four years through corporate training and development programs.
- Established computerized tracking system for waste removal program.
- Monitored air and water pollution levels for three-county territory.
- Developed and implemented plans for corrective measures on air and water emissions.
- Instituted tougher standards for emissions voluntarily.
- Trained field engineers in pollution evaluation and control.

Engineering Technician, American Marine Drilling Corporation, 1992 to 1997
San Diego, California
- Designed and directed drilling operations from start-up to dismantling.
- Trained in hazardous waste shipping and chemical containment.
- Monitored marine geophysical research reports and incorporated relevant information into design and operations plans.

EDUCATION
B.S., Petrophysical Engineering, 1991
Colorado Institute of Mineral Science and Technology - Mountain Park

Patrick J. Allan

17 East Moreland Drive
Chicago, Illinois 60611
Tel: (312) 555-2298
E-mail: p.j.allen@xxx.com

Registration

Licensed Professional Engineer, State of Illinois
Certified Environmental Professional, National

Recent Accomplishments

- Served as project manager for the successful completion of a comprehensive, integrated, solid waste management project for Will County, south of Chicago.
- Assisted in the preparation and implementation of a land-use development plan for the state of Illinois, in cooperation with the Land Development Commission, the Environmental Protection League, and the Federal Bureau of Land Management.
- Prepared and directed engineering feasibility study, including environmental impact statement, for siting of water treatment facility.

Employment History

1995–2002	**Templeton Environmental Consultants, Inc.** 452 East Stewart Avenue, Suite 112 Chicago, Illinois 60612 *Senior Environmental Engineering Consultant*
1991–1995	**M. W. N. Engineering Associates, Ltd.** Parker Building, Suite 2600 24th and Madison Chicago, Illinois 60602 *Engineer - Hydrologist*
1987–1991	**Tensor Industries, Inc.** 144 West Marquam Chicago, Illinois 60626 *Engineering Technician*

Education

1987	L.P.E. Course, Central Technical Institute
1986	B.S., Geological Engineering, Wheaton College

References available on request.

• JONATHAN HOOPER •

7728 S. Coruna Street • Santa Fe, NM 87502 • 505-555-2497

• CURRENT OBJECTIVE •

Project management position with an environmental technologies consulting firm.

• SUMMARY OF QUALIFICATIONS •

Expertise in the areas of waste-to-energy and waste-recovery technology solutions, recycling technology, review and preparation of environmental impact statements, testing and analysis of groundwater levels and flow, and electric power generation technologies. Excellent written and oral communications skills and thorough knowledge of environmental regulations for federal and state policy makers.

• RECENT PROJECT EXPERIENCE •

- Project Manager for Santa Fe Environmental Systems Waste-to-Energy Feasibility Study—Prepared an analysis of the solid waste management practices of the Santa Fe regional facility, coupled with an environmental assessment of a potential site to determine the feasibility of developing a waste-to-energy facility in Lamy, New Mexico. Developed program design for study.
- Consultant/Project Manager for Sante Fe Department of Sanitation—Prepared a feasibility study (environmental fatal flaws, geotechnical analysis, engineering constraints, hydrogeologic analysis) for the proposed redevelopment of the closed San Felipe Landfill for use as an ash residue disposal site for the city's solid waste incinerators and proposed waste-to-energy facilities.
- Lead Environmental Scientist for New Mexico Transfer Station—Developed permit documents and environmental assessments for a solid waste transfer station in southern New Mexico.
- Lead Environmental Analyst for the County Energy Management Committee—Designed study to perform environmental impact comparative analysis of current coal generators versus waste-to-energy incinerator-generators. Study published in national professional journal.

• WORK HISTORY •

1998 - present:	Consultant, Enso Environmental Associates, Santa Fe
1996 - 1998:	Hydrologist, New Mexico Department of Energy, Albuquerque
1992 - 1996:	Research Associate, University of New Mexico, Albuquerque

• EDUCATION •

1992: Bachelor's degree in Hydrology Engineering
University of New Mexico, Albuquerque

References on request.

Trent Howard
149 NE Goshen Drive
Fredericksburg, VA 22405
703/555-6265

EMPLOYMENT OBJECTIVE
Environmental consultant for water resources management organization.

EDUCATION
M.S., Water Resources Engineering
Virginia Technical Institute, 2001

B.S., Civil Engineering (minor in Water Resource Engineering)
Purdue University, 1988

WORK HISTORY AND EXPERIENCE
Research Associate, Virginia Technical Institute, 1998 to present
*Hired as associate to Research and Consulting Division of VTI to work on
a variety of special projects, including:*

- Georgia Rivers Study: Investigate navigability of the streams and rivers within the civil works area; under contract to the U.S. Army Corps of Engineers, Savannah, Georgia.
- Alaska Rivers Study: Investigate navigability of the streams and rivers crossed by the Trans-Alaska Oil Pipeline; under contract to the U.S. Army Corps of Engineers, Alaska District.
- Wetlands Study: Perform comparative analysis of methods of identifying freshwater wetlands; under contract to the U.S. Army Corps of Engineers, Adirondack District.
- Upper Roanoke River Basin Study: Investigate navigability, water flow, and water quality of waters of the Upper Roanoke River Basin; under contract to the State of Virginia, Department of Water Resources.
- Headwater Pilot Program: Conduct hydrologic analysis of small headwater streams to determine selection of cfs location along the Upper James River, Virginia; under contract to the State of Virginia, Department of Water Resources.

MEMBERSHIPS
Water Resources Institute of Virginia
Institute of Environmental Sciences and Technology
American Water Resources Association

Complete references provided on request.

PAUL R. BROWN

325 S. Grant Ave. • Bellingham, WA 98225 • (206) 555-2284

OBJECTIVE

To obtain employment as an environmental specialist consultant

SUMMARY OF EXPERIENCE

- Participated in the Oil Spill Response and Effects Task Force, 1995–2001.
- Tracked oil spill research activities in the United States, Canada, and Europe for environmental action organization.
- Served on a panel for the Environmental Conservation Association's Oil Spill Response Workshop in Edinburgh, Scotland, 2000.
- Led a rescue team during the emergency response to Exxon Valdez oil spill in Alaska.
- Participated in joint meetings with environmentalists and officials from four major U.S. petroleum companies to develop standard cooperative response procedures to oil spills.
- Participated in on-scene response at four major oil spills (Valdez, Lima Refinery, Glacier Bay, and Nestucca Bay).
- Conducted laboratory research on birds and animals killed in the Valdez spill.
- Developed database management procedures for tracking impact of Valdez spill and preparation of statistics vital to legislative lobbying programs.
- Five years of experience as wildlife biologist for government agency involved with research and wildlife management.

EMPLOYMENT HISTORY

Environmental Specialist
Oil Spill Response and Effects Task Force, Washington, DC, 1995–2001

Wildlife Biologist
Washington Bureau of Fisheries and Wildlife, 1990–1995

Volunteer
Greenpeace Institute, London, England, 1988–1989

EDUCATION

Bachelor of Science, Wildlife Biology
Stanford University, California, 1988

REFERENCES

Provided upon request

GENE BRUNK P.O. Box 133 Newport, RI 02840 401-555-4603

OBJECTIVE
Project management position with water quality control agency.

PROJECT EXPERIENCE
- Lake Michigan Regional Assessment Study for the National Commission on Water Quality: Evaluated the benefits and costs of the Water Pollution Control Act Amendments of 1991 for the water quality of Lake Michigan.
- Developed toxic pollutant control strategies for urban areas for the U.S. Environmental Protection Agency.
- Analyzed proposed effluent limitations for fluoride from the semiconductor and crystal and crystal products subcategories of the electrical and electronics products industry.
- Assessed current pollutant loadings from the iron and steel industry to selected rivers; determined current and projected water quality following implementation of BAT effluent limitations.
- Estimated direct discharge loadings into various major rivers leading to Lake Erie for the organic chemicals and plastics and synthetic fibers industries.
- Analyzed proposed copper effluent limitations and potential criteria violations for 12 priority pollutants resulting from discharges of air preheater wash and boiler fireside wash effluents by the steam electric power industry in Illinois.
- National Coastal Pollutant Inventory for the National Oceanic and Atmospheric Administration: Investigated point and nonpoint water pollutant discharges.

EMPLOYMENT HISTORY
Principal Investigator, Water Quality Division
Westerly Engineering, Providence, RI, 1994 to present

Research Scientist
Rhode Island Institute of Technology, Providence, 1990 to 1994

EDUCATION
B.S. in Chemical Engineering, Rhode Island Institute of Technology, 1990

REFERENCES
Provided upon request.

CARMEN S. DOMINI

753 South Main Street
Melrose, Massachusetts 02176
Cellular Phone: 508-555 8229
E-mail: carmen.domini@xxx.com

OBJECTIVE
To obtain employment as a site engineer for an electric power company.

EXPERIENCE
Site Reconnaissance Study
Performed study to site a steam power plant on Long Island. Task Manager for Long Island Lighting Company in Long Island, New York, 1996–2001.

Engineering Design Project
Developed and designed a 330-MW, coal-fired electric generating facility and appurtenant structures. Lead Environmental Hydrologist for the Colorado Power Company in Golden, Colorado, 1990–1996.

Northern California Project
Developed engineering design and permitting information for the construction of a major fossil-fuel-fired electric generating facility. Lead Environmental Hydrologist for Public Service Company of California in Eureka, California, 1986–1990.

Occidental Geothermal
Conducted site analysis and developed a permitting document for the construction of a steam/electric geothermal power plant in the Geysers area of California. Environmental Hydrologist for Occidental Corporation in Geysers, California, 1985–1986.

San Francisco Bay Regional Power Plan
Developed an engineering feasibility study for electric power generation in the Bay Area. Lead Environmental Scientist/Assistant Project Manager for the California Power Authority in San Francisco, California, 1981–1985.

EDUCATION
University of Massachusetts, Amherst
Bachelor of Science, Civil Engineering, 1981
Major area of concentration: Hydrology

REFERENCES
Provided upon request.

VINCENT CARRINGTON

90 West Bridge Street   Buffalo, New York 14201
(716) 555-4473   V.Carrington@xxx.com

OBJECTIVE
Management position with engineering consulting firm.

PROJECT MANAGEMENT EXPERIENCE
EMPLOYMENT HISTORY
DEIS Manager for SSGR Corporation in Buffalo, New York

"Regent" residential subdivision - Prepared a draft environmental impact statement for a 280-unit condominium complex with special emphasis on water supply, wastewater disposal, traffic, and aesthetics. 1995 to present.

Lead Environmental Scientist for Carson Properties, Inc. in Albany, New York

Carson Properties Feasibility Study - Prepared an environmental engineering feasibility document for the development of a residential subdivision, with emphasis on water supply and wastewater disposal. 1992 to 1995.

Lead Environmental, Scientist for the Breckenridge Corporation in Albany, New York

Sterling Forest Master Plan - Provided technical review of baseline and alternative action studies for the development of a major land holding in southeastern New York State. 1992.

Project Manager, United States Postal Service, Real Estate Division in Waterbury, Connecticut

Prepared an environmental assessment (NEPA) for the proposed expansion of the New Bedford General Mail Facility in New Bedford, Connecticut, including a wetland delineation report pursuant to the *Federal Wetland Manual for Identifying and Delineating Jurisdictional Wetlands*. 1990 to 1991.

Project Manager, U.S. Environmental Protection Agency in Brooklyn, New York

Prepared radon surveys for major corporate buildings in Brooklyn, New York. 1985 to 1990.

EDUCATION
Bachelor of Science, Chemistry, 1983
University of Connecticut

References on Request

SUSANA MARSTON

14555 Birch Lane
Durham, New Hampshire 03824
Daytime: 603-555-3892, ext. 2899

Education
Bachelor of Science in Biology, 1992, University of New Hampshire, Durham

Experience
Scientific Technician, Department of Forest Biology, University of New Hampshire, Durham
Study the impact of acid deposition on coastal forests. Design and conduct analyses on tree leaf surfaces, foliar elements, and tree ring morphology. Process fog and rain samples for ionic analyses. Install and operate weather monitoring systems on remote island sites. Train site operators to collect samples. Process, analyze, and prepare data for scientific publication. Maintain laboratory and supervise personnel. Gain expertise in scanning and transmitting electron microscopy, darkroom techniques, statistical analyses, mainframe and microcomputer work, and image analysis systems. 1996–present

Laboratory Assistant, Department of Entomology, University of New Hampshire, Durham
Monitored the effects of acid rain on the developmental stages of aquatic insects and studied pesticide effectiveness on spruce budworm. Subjected caddis flies to artificially acidified streams and applied sublethal levels of several chemicals on spruce budworm to measure survival rate, egg production, and pupal weights. Extracted RNA from caddis flies. Maintained stocks of experimental insects. Processed data and supervised summer college students. 1995

Field and Research Technician, Department of Entomology, University of New Hampshire, Durham
Assisted in several studies on the success of spruce budworm pesticides and their effects on nontarget organisms. Collected and sorted aquatic invertebrates from streams containing pesticides. Collected spruce budworm invertebrates from streams containing pesticides. Collected spruce budworm samples from remote treatment sites. Processed data. 1992–1994

Technical Skills
Scanning Electron Microscopes: Amray AMR 100 and JEOL J06400; Transmitting Electron Microscopes: Philip EM201; Computer programs: Statistical Analysis System (SAS), Harvard Graphics, Microsoft Office 2000

References
Available upon request

Kirk R. Helprin

900 Woodlawn Drive
Alpena, Michigan 49707
517-555-5524

Objective

A position in environmental education

Relevant Experience

Messier Environmental Education Center, Alpena, Michigan
Guide, 2001. Taught middle school students natural history, local history, and human environmental impact during summer resident camp programs and school-year science camp programs.

Blue Hills Bird Observatory, Ellsworth, Maine
Field Ornithologist, summers 1997–2000. Conducted common loon research: banded loons to assess population dynamics (site fidelity, minimum survival rate) and behavior, collected blood and feather samples to measure environmental contaminants. Demonstrated common loon capture technique at North American Loon Society Meeting, Ellsworth, Maine, August 1999.

Raptor Banding Assistant, 1997–1998. Conducted owl, hawk, and passerine banding, including monitoring and removal of birds from mist nets; banding; and collecting weight, wing and tail length, and age data. Presented weekly lectures on raptor natural history.

JOLA, Inc., Washington, DC
Research Assistant, September 1996–June 1997. Worked on projects for the U.S. Environmental Protection Agency (EPA) in areas of environmental policy and risk assessment: develop a risk assessment guidance manual for the Superfund program; identified indicators of environmental quality, status, and trends; developed a wildlife exposure factors handbook; developed EPA policy for the protection of biodiversity; and analyzed ecological indicators of environmental progress in the Superfund program. Assisted in development of EPA documents. Conducted research, interviews, and telephone surveys. Reviewed literature, wrote summaries, and incorporated information into reports. Developed briefing materials for management.

U.S. Forest Service, Blue Mountain National Forest, Lexington, Kentucky
Biological Technician, summer 1996. Conducted stream habitat and fish population surveys to be used for the management of the national forest's fishery and forest resources.

Education

B.A., Biology/Environmental Studies, 1996, Bates College, Lewiston, Maine
Participated in four-week workshop on teaching techniques, Messier Center, 2001

References available on request

Mark Anaya
3892 Otis Lane • Monterey, CA 93940 • 408-555-8889

Objective
To obtain a challenging position as a field/research biologist.

Work History
1996–present. Point Lobos Bird Observatory (PLBO), Point Lobos State Reserve, Monterey, CA. Field Biologist.
- Monitor and conduct census of cetaceans, sea, shore, and land birds on and around waters of PLBO.
- Assist PLBO biologists in monitoring great white shark activity to examine population density, individual phenotype, and predation strategy.
- Assisted pinniped project by recording tagged and wounded animals, particularly northern elephant seals. Documented development of social hierarchy, marked unknown breeding-age individuals, and monitored all breeding activity.

1995. Institute of Birds, Great Smoky Mountains National Park, TN. Field Biologist.
- Established six permanent sites within specific habitats where data is collected to monitor avian productivity and survivorship (MAPS program), including operating standardized mist nets and conducting point counts.

1994. PLBO, Bitterwater Field Station, CA. Field Biologist.
- Operated mist nets for long-term research designed to gather and analyze critical data on migration, productivity, and survivorship of land birds, and to relate data to environmental changes.
- Presented interpretive programs to schools, universities, and interested environmental organizations.
- Conducted detailed monitoring of lives, territories, and nesting activities of known-age, individually color-banded population of four coexisting, nonmigratory land bird species. Examined patterns of heredity, fitness, age, experience, behavior, and lifetime reproductive success.

1993. The Environmental Institute, Port Orford, OR. Intern.
- Assisted projects with alternative technology in areas of resource management, forest ecology, and sustainable agriculture.
- Provided environmental education programs to children.

1992. U.S. Fish and Wildlife Service, White Mountain National Forest, VT. Intern.
- Studied mosquito populations, life cycles; submitted data to effect cessation of pesticide spraying by county vector control. Documented shifts in mosquito predator populations.

Education
University of California, Santa Barbara, B.S. - Biology, 1993.

Margarita Salinas

3890 Piñon Avenue • Carlsbad, New Mexico 88220 • 505-555-5765

Objective

A position in ecological research, focusing on public education and policy development

Work Experience

Interpretive Ranger, Carlsbad Caverns National Park, New Mexico, 1995–present
- Present original nature walks and cave tours, geology talks, and slide shows on local ecosystems to the public.
- Service as asssistant editor of park newsletter.
- Designed and implemented a water quality study of the park's water resources.
- Designed and developed a visitor interpretive center to provide a simulation of the cavern interior for visitors unable to explore caverns and to lower visitor impact on caverns.

Research Assistant, Smithsonian Tropical Research Institute, Barro Rico Island, Costa Rica, 1993–1995
- Participated in extensive habitat analysis study in cooperation with government of Costa Rica.
- Identified and gathered data on flora; collected and catalogued samples; maintained detailed journal and natural history notebook; provided ecological information to visitors to the center.

Field Assistant and Intern, New England Ecological Center, Warren, Maine, summer 1992
- Designed and implemented independent field project comparing two ecosystems.
- Helped design and conduct group field experiments.
- Analyzed and interpreted ecosystem-level functions of natural communities at five inland riparian sites.

Education

Yale University, New Haven, Connecticut
B.S. in Environmental Biology, cum laude, 1992

Memberships

Society for Conservation Biology
The Wilderness Society
Greenpeace
National Spelunkers Association

References available on request

Felice Anthony

3442 South Bridge Road • North Tonawanda, NY 14120
716-555-1093

Objective

A management position in environmental chemical research

Education

M.A., State University of New York, Albany
Chemistry, 1998

B.A., Cornell University, Ithaca, NY
Environmental Studies, Policy, and Management, 1996

Experience

Staff Research Specialist, Arizona State University, Tempe
Environmental Toxicology Institute, 1998–present
- Developed and oversaw procurement and setup of planned instrumentation and laboratory (Europa Scientific elemental analyis/isotope ratio mass spectrometer system, featuring automated analysis capabilities for isotopes of hydrogen, oxygen, nitrogen, and carbon in solid, liquid, and gaseous samples). Developed protocols. Supervised and trained users. Assisted in administering facility.

Teaching Assistant, State University of New York, Albany
Department of Chemistry, 1996–1998
- Taught freshman chemistry classes. Evaluated and assigned grades for examinations. Taught and monitored laboratory classes and graded scientific reports.

Research Assistant, New York Public Interest Research Group, Ithaca
1993–1996
- Completed extensive surveys of the general public by phone and in person. Compiled results to analyze the environmental awareness of a cross section of the population of New York state. Acted as liaison with national and regional Public Interest Research Group branches in the area of public education and environmental issues. Organized local survey efforts.

Skills

- Extensive experience with mass spectrometry, computer programming, and data analysis.
- Wide-ranging experience with all equipment in an elemental analysis/isotope ratio mass spectrometer facility
- Expertise with physiological methods involving stable isotopes
- Programming experience in statistical analyses

References
Available on request

JOEY P. MULBERRY

334 SE 12th   Department of Geography
Austin, TX 78710   University of Texas, Austin
512-555-3892   512-555-8800, Ext. 43

OBJECTIVE
A position in the private sector involving water resources and public policy.

EDUCATION
Ph.D. Candidate
Department of Geography, University of Texas, Austin. Thesis topic: An Implementation Analysis of the Coastal Texas Power Planning Council's Regional Plans. Expected completion date: Spring 2002.

M.S.
Department of Geography, University of Minnesota, Duluth. Thesis: Perception of Recreational Lake Quality. August 1997.

B.S.
Department of Geography, State University of New York, Albany. Physical Geography. May 1994.

WORK EXPERIENCE
Faculty Research Assistant
Texas Water Resources Research Institute, University of Texas, Austin.
10/2000–present.
Provide evaluation and technical assistance to government agencies in Texas that are developing and implementing nonpoint sources monitoring plans under the 1995 Clean Water Act Section 319 National Monitoring Program.

Instructor
University of Texas Continuing Higher Education Program, Austin.
Department of Geography course: Environmental Conservation.
9/2000–1/2001.

Graduate Research Assistant
Texas Water Resources Research Institute, University of Texas, Austin.
2/2000–9/2000.

Page 1 of 2

Instructor
Department of Geography, University of Texas, Austin.
Course: Geography of the Western World.
9/1998–6/2000.

Teaching Assistant
Department of Geography, University of Texas, Austin.
Course: Department Seminar Series.
1/1998–6/1998.

Lab Instructor
Department of Geography, University of Texas, Austin.
Course: Cartography.
9/1997–12/1997.

PROFESSIONAL ORGANIZATIONS

Association of American Geographers (AAG)
AAG Water Resources Specialty Group
Association of Gulf Coast Geographers
American Water Resources Association (AWRA)
AWRA Student Activities Committee

References Available

Laurel Hightower

8889 Northwest Barclay Street • Portland, Maine 04401
207-555-9882 • Laurel.Hightower@xxx.com

Objective
A position in marine resources involving community development and policy

Education
University of Maine, Orono, 1997–present
Candidate for master's degree in Marine Resource Science, College of Ecology

University of New Hampshire, Durham, 1991–1996
Coursework in Physiology, Botany, Oceanography, Ecology, Computer Science, Biology, Biochemistry, and Environmental Law

University of Massachusetts, Boston, 1987–1991
Bachelor of arts degree in Comparative Literature, minor in Education

Work Experience
Project Assistant, Revitalization of Two Small Communities' Waterfronts, A National Demonstration Project UMO Extension/Sea Grant, 1997–present.
- Manage the logistics of community meetings
- Maintain day-to-day contacts with community
- Assist in agenda development and meeting facilitation
- Perform community surveys and analyze results
- Secure development permits
- Identify potential funding and technical resources
- Assist in planning and designing workshops

Biology Technician, New England Labs, United States Forest Service, Durham, NH, 1994–1996 (seasonal)
- Used Hankin & Reeves methodology to conduct stream survey work.
- Identified fish
- Determined habitat and substrate type
- Identified and typed vegetation
- Collected data

Other Experience
Volunteer, New England Development and Marine Planning Commission, 1995–present
- Assist in development, planning, and support services of regionwide environmental coalition involved in revitalization, economic, and environmental issues

References
Available on request

Karel P. Margolise

2893 Puma Street   Davis, CA 95616   (916) 555-3923

Objective

Position as fisheries biologist involved in treaty rights and resource management

Experience

Fisheries Research Assistant, 1999–2001
Indian Forest Management Assessment Team
- Participated in a congressionally mandated study of the condition and management of Indian forest trust lands.
- Conducted site visits, interviews, and assessments at over 15 Indian reservations and native Alaska corporations.
- Synthesized information and wrote reports focusing on the condition and management of fisheries resources on Indian forest trust lands.
- Assisted in writing and editing the final report.
- Coordinated with other team members regarding information distribution, scheduling, site visit organization, and other aspects of the study.

Biological Technician, 1998–1999
United States Forest Service, Forestry Laboratory, Pacific Northwest Research Station, Olympia, WA
- Conducted riparian survey and collected data for calculating wood volume.
- Surveyed stream to study fish habitat.
- Gathered data on fish populations using electroshock.
- Organized and entered data.
- Assisted with various mapping projects, including projects for the Gang of Four.

Scientific Technician, 1997–1998
Harper-Ray Environmental Consultants, Tacoma, WA
- Surveyed specific animal species along proposed pipeline route.
- Surveyed and collected data for instream flow incremental methodology studies.
- Organized and entered data.
- Assisted in preparing reports for clients.

Scientific Technician, 1995–1997
Washington Department of Wildlife, Seattle, WA
- Recorded catch data from treaty Indian steelhead harvest.
- Assisted in monitoring treaty Indian fishing regulations.
- Compiled current fishing regulations.

Education

Bachelor of Science in Biology and Environmental Policy
Willamette University, Salem, Oregon - 1995

CLARA B. DUNNING

186 Montgomery Street
Iowa City, IA 52242
319-555-2341
C.B.Dunning@xxx.com

OBJECTIVE

To obtain a field research position with an environmental consulting firm

EDUCATION

B.S., Environmental Science and Chemistry
University of Kansas, Lawrence, 1996

WORK EXPERIENCE

Field Biologist, Milman, Inc., Iowa City, IA

Lead crew on four-year avian research project examining the effects of a new pesticide for golf course use. Supervise, train, and schedule research crew consisting of two biologists and 10 technicians whose responsibilities include mist-netting, censusing, carcass searching, and residue sampling. Conduct quality assurance checks on all field procedures and data collected. Summarize data and write reports. 1998 - present

Field Technician II, The Institute of Environmental Toxicology, University of Iowa, Iowa City

Led team of avian census and carcass search teams as part of a project studying the effects of an agricultural pesticide in southwestern Iowa. Supervised, trained, and scheduled avian census and carcass search teams. Tested efficiency of carcass searching. Conducted quality assurance checks on all field procedures and data collected. Collected avian census data and trapped birds to be used in radio telemetry research. 1997 - 1998

Lab Assistant, Environmental Studies Department, University of Iowa, Iowa City

Prepared labs for a variety of courses (Chemistry, Anatomy, Cell Biology, Ecology, Toxic Environments, Botany). Prepared laboratory solutions and ran equipment such as pH meters, autoclaves, stills, and scales. Trained, supervised, and scheduled other student assistants. Supervised the maintenance of laboratory animals and greenhouse. 1993 - 1997

George Montaine

996 Poplar Drive   Minneapolis, MN 55401
612-555-4576   g.montaine@xxx.com

Objective
Obtain an entry-level position relating to environmental policy or research

Education
University of Minnesota, Morris
B.S., 2000, Resource Development
College of Agriculture and Natural Resources
> Relevant coursework: Environmental Impact Assessment, Management of Environmental Issues, Natural Resource Analysis Techniques, Resource Development Policy, Conservation of Natural Resources, Community and Regional Development, Land Economics, Environmental Permits and Regulation, Water Resource Development, Chemistry, Physics, Geology, Biology, Geography, Soil Science, Ecology

Job Experience
Hartford-Morris, Inc., Minneapolis, MN, 1999-present
Assistant Manager
- Supervise employees in two stores during daily restaurant operations
- Handle accounts payable and administer petty cash for six stores and compute payroll for over 100 employees on a weekly basis
- Developed campaign for public awareness and recycling that was implemented at all company restaurants
- Monitored on-site safety procedures at several restaurants

Activities
- University of Minnesota Annual Leadership Conference
- Resource Development Undergraduate Association
- Project Recycle Organization
- National Audubon Society Conservation Committee

Special Interests and Skills
- Broad interest in meteorology, worldwide physical geography
- Extensive ornithological experience with the National Audubon Society
- Computer experience with Waterloo BASIC, WordPerfect, Microsoft Word, ArcInfo, Geographic Information Systems, Quattro Pro

Ricardo Particlo

389 Belmont Street
San Francisco, CA 94105
415-555-1903

Objective

A management position in the private or nonprofit sector involving wildlife refuges, habitat, or rehabilitation.

Work Experience

Assistant Regional Director, Don Edwards San Francisco Bay National Wildlife Refuge, Fremont, CA
1999–present

Project director for the wildlife complex, comprised of eight national wildlife refuges in northern California. The refuges span 300 miles and vary widely in purpose, habitat type, and wildlife. Over 400,000 visit the complex annually for wildlife observation, interpretive tours, photography, canoeing, boating, biking, picnicking, hunting, trapping, and fishing.

Responsibilities

- Develop refuge policy and coordinate technical activities of the refuge programs with numerous government agencies and representatives of special interest groups, as well as extensive coordination with media.
- Plan, direct, and administer a complex operation that includes directing the maintenance of buildings, grounds, and equipment; planning projects in construction and rehabilitation; managing fire control, grazing, and haying operations; managing a law enforcement program; and administering operations associated with all fiscal, personnel, and property operations.

Special Skills

- Supervision of large, multidisciplinary staff.
- Resolution of complex natural resource problems involving impact on the public and economic use of refuge lands.
- Knowledge of goals, objectives, legal/regulatory requirements and processes concerning the management of a diverse group of national wildlife refuges.
- Ability to meet and deal with individuals and groups from varying backgrounds and with varying interests.
- Ability to communicate both orally and in writing.

Page 1 of 2

**Refuge Manager, Northern Redwood Refuge, Eureka, CA
1990–1999**
- Project leader for refuge that supports peak populations of half a million waterfowl and public use activities such as wildlife observation, interpretive tours, photography, hunting, and fishing.

Responsibilities
- Planned, directed, and administered operations in accordance with established management plans, policies, objectives, and environmental and cultural resource mandates.
- Developed refuge policy and coordinated technical activities with government agencies and special interest groups.
- Designed and implemented wildlife and public use studies.

**Wildlife Biologist, California Department of Fish and Wildlife, San Francisco
1982–1990**
- Designed, supervised, and analyzed research of wetland bird species, including studies of migration, mating, habitat use, and population management.

**Nature Interpreter, Marston T. Fairweather Park, Monterey, CA
1980–1982**
- Led interpretive walks for visitors to wetland refuge. Presented talks and demonstrations.

Education

M.S., Wildlife Biology, specializing in Marine Biology
University of California, Santa Cruz
1988

B.S., Wildlife Biology
University of California, Berkeley
1980

References available.

MARY BELGROSSO

68 Evergreen Drive
Rutland, Vermont 05701

802-555-2983

PROFESSIONAL OBJECTIVES

Field researcher in areas of wildlife biology, vertebrate zoology, or ornithology.
Interpretor of natural history within state or national park systems.

QUALIFICATIONS

- Identification of wildlife in field
- Netting and banding of live birds and animals
- Research in field observation/collection projects
- Familiarity with many facets of sanctuary management
- Interpretation of history/natural history and ecology in park settings
- Designing and implementing formal discussions/presentations on various historical and natural topics
- Photographic and computer/word processing skills
- Familiarity with law enforcement principles and techniques as related to parks and preserves

EDUCATION

Bachelor of Science in Biology, graduated cum laude, 2000
University of New Hampshire, Durham

Certificate of Completion, National Park Service Seasonal Law Enforcement
Ranger Training Program, Western Community College, Sylva, North Carolina,
1992. Hours completed: 460

VOLUNTEER EXPERIENCE

U.S. Fish and Wildlife Service
Hawaii Biological Research Station
Research Assistant, June–Dec 2001
- Participated in endangered bird recovery program. Searched in field for nest sites, analyzed contents of nests, set up mist nets. Captured, measured, banded, and released Hawaiian passerines. Established new study transects, input data, and maintained minor equipment.

Rolling Hills Wildlife Refuge, New Hampshire
Research Assistant, 1999–2000
- Conducted waterfowl survey at refuge. Identified species and reported numbers of waterfowl to refuge staff.

WORK EXPERIENCE

National Park Service
Mammoth Hot Springs, Yellowstone National Park
Interpretive Ranger, June–Sept 2002
- Organized and led guided tours. Ensured visitor safety by trailing tours. Wrote and conducted short talks on historical/natural subjects. Staffed information desk and presented audiovisual programs at visitor center.

Everglades National Park, Florida
Park Ranger, Oct 2000–April 2001
- Collected camping fees, assigned sites, prepared large deposits, patrolled campground for compliance with regulations at park's largest campground.

MEMBERSHIPS
Sierra Club
Oceanic Society
Smithsonian Institution
The Humane Society of the United States
Natural Resources Defense Council
National Audubon Society

REFERENCES AVAILABLE ON REQUEST

Sample Cover Letters

This chapter contains many sample cover letters for people pursuing a wide variety of jobs and careers in the environmental fields.

There are many different styles of cover letters in terms of layout, level of formality, and presentation of information. These samples also represent people with varying amounts of education and work experience. Choose one cover letter or borrow elements from several different cover letters to help you construct your own.

Paul E. Morrison
34 Tulane Drive
Des Moines, IA 50317

January 22, 20__

Mr. Armand Summers
Environmental Associates
14 Veterans Boulevard
Des Moines, IA 50309

Dear Mr. Summers:

I am writing to inquire about employment opportunities with
Environmental Associates. Enclosed you will find my resume outlining
my professional experience.

I am a registered civil engineer with over seven years of civil/environ-
mental marketing experience in the environmental construction products
industry with Semlar Environmental Systems (Semlar structural
geogrids) and Crown Zellerbach Corporation (nonwoven geotextiles).
Prior experience includes nine years as a project/construction manager
for Bechtel Engineering and six years as a project/refinery engineer in
the oil industry.

I hope to obtain a regional marketing and/or technical support position
within the private sector. My extensive contacts in the Midwest with
environmental engineering consultants, regulatory agencies, and landfill
owners/operators offer the prospect of generating new business for your
firm.

Thank you kindly for your assistance. I look forward to talking with
you further.

Sincerely,

Paul E. Morrison, P.E.
Enclosure

Walter Beckett
88 Marshall Street • Williston, ND 58801 • (701) 555-2338

March 15, 20__

Personnel Division
Weston/Havens, Inc.
745 NW Wall Street
P.O. Box 218, Dept. PE 8
Denver, CO 80209

RE: Employment in Environmental/Waste Management (Hazardous/Solid Waste)/Regulation Compliance

To Whom It May Concern:

I am pleased to submit my resume in response to your advertised positions in the latest edition of *Environment Update*. The resume outlines my experience in industrial and hazardous waste management, regulations, compliance, and environmental technology.

I offer over 12 years of experience in environmental technology, project management, technical standards development, and waste management. Most recently I held a position as a project manager of environmental technology at the U.S. Environmental Protection Agency (EPA). Prior to the EPA, I worked for 5 years at Infirion, Inc., a subsidiary of the Infirion Company of Lexington, Massachusetts. My duties included care of industrial wastes, effluent treatment, recycling, and regulation compliance (Reg-309, Clean Air Act, hazardous wastes, and MISA).

Positions Desired: Senior engineering/project management
Salary Desired: $60,000 range, but negotiable
Locations: Open, but prefer southwest, southeast, or south-central United States

I can be reached by phone or at the E-mail address listed above. I am happy to make arrangements to travel to Denver to meet with you and discuss the position further. Thank you for your consideration, and I look forward to talking with you soon.

Sincerely,

Walter Beckett

Margaret Samuelson

3131 Mountain Drive   Longmont, CO 80501   (303) 555-2435

May 8, 20__

Susan Franklin
Personnel Director
Specialist Books
P.O. Box 2362
Denver, CO 80235

Dear Ms. Franklin:

Please accept the enclosed resume and letters of recommendation in application for the Senior Editor position with the Environmental Science Division of Specialist Books. I am responding to the position announcement listed in the March 26 edition of *Publishers Weekly*.

Currently I hold the position of Managing Editor of the University of Colorado Press, with full responsibility for acquisitions, development, design, and production. The position has been an extremely rewarding one, but statewide budget cuts within higher education have resulted in the indefinite closure of the press.

Therefore, I would like to put my energy and extensive publishing background to work for Specialist Books in your Environmental Science Division. Approximately 65 percent of the titles I published with the UC Press were of a scientific or technical nature, and I gained additional editorial experience in the field as Editorial Assistant for the Environmental Studies Department of the university.

I would be happy to forward copies of relevant publications—both initial manuscripts and final publications—as examples of my editorial work. I also would appreciate an opportunity to discuss the position with you personally. I can be reached at the above number after working hours and on weekends, and at (303) 555-0429, ext. 23, during the week.

I look forward to receiving your call and thank you in advance for your consideration.

Yours sincerely,

Margaret Samuelson

Margarita Salinas

3890 Piñon Avenue
Carlsbad, New Mexico 88220
505-555-5765

June 16, 20__

Calvin Falkenberry
Director of Educational Programs
El Malpais National Conservation Area
620 East Santa Fe Avenue
Grants, New Mexico 87020

Dear Mr. Falkenberry:

Thank you for taking the time to talk with me yesterday about the Associate Director of Environmental Education position currently open at El Malpais. Your sincere enthusiasm for the program has prompted me to wish to join this endeavor and I have therefore enclosed my resume in application for the job.

For the past seven years I have worked as an interpretive ranger at the Carlsbad Caverns National Park, where I was responsible for developing and presenting nature walks, cave tours, geology talks, and slide shows on local ecosystems to the public. I was very much involved in developing new programs, and in some sense served as a de facto director in the absence of any other supervision for the program. I would enjoy a position with the kind of support network you described and the freedom it would allow for developing truly innovative and challenging educational programs.

I look forward to talking with you again soon, and I hope that my resume persuades you of my qualifications for this position. In addition, I speak fluent Spanish, which has often been helpful in my work at Carlsbad.

I would be delighted to travel to Grants to meet with you in person and tour the facilities. Many thanks for your kindness and consideration.

Sincerely,

Margarita Salinas

Darius G. W. Harms

3485 Plainfield Road
Lincoln, Nebraska 68573
402-555-9287
DariusHarms@xxx.com

August 23, 20__

Jonathan Parker
Engineering Division Director
State of Nebraska
P.O. Box 5678
Lincoln, Nebraska 68570

Dear Mr. Parker:

Please accept this letter and the enclosed resume in application for the Environmental Project Supervisor position announced February 25, 2002.

I believe my extensive background with recycling equipment and waste management meets or exceeds the qualifications of the current position. I have served both as a senior project manager and as a supervisor with responsibility for 120 workers.

For my part, I would like to put my expertise and experience to work for the benefit of the environment where, as stated in your position description, livability and quality form the guiding values. Too often in the corporate world, the demand for higher profit margins takes precedence over innovative developments and worker safety. My experience in this field will allow me to achieve desired results in the most efficient manner possible, thus cutting costs and increasing productivity.

Please review the enclosed resume and call me at the number above. I would like to discuss the position and what my talent and experience can bring to your department.

Yours truly,

Darius Harms

Stewart A. Zalasar

Environmental Consultant
2356 West 13th Street
Madison, WI 53701
Telephone and Fax: (608) 555-9534

October 31, 20__

Environmental Industries Worldwide
P.O. Box 145B
Madison, WI 53709

Dear Personnel Manager:

I understand that your firm specializes in locating and employing recycling, environmental, and safety professionals for industrial clients. I was an environmental manager for BP America Utilities until December of 2000, when I left to expand my practice as an independent consultant. I would now like to return to the corporate world in a senior environmental management position or into a major environmental consulting firm.

Enclosed is a copy of my resume. You will see that I have over 10 years of experience in the environmental field that covers a number of disciplines. Areas of concentration include water quality management, environmental auditing, regulatory work, spill emergency preparedness, and environmental assessment. I would be interested in discussing with you both current opportunities and longer term prospects. Thank you for your consideration.

Yours truly,

Stewart A. Zalasar

Erika Waters

789A Baker Avenue
Jacksonville, FL 32254
904-555-2432

December 21, 20__

Elena Turner-White
EcoSpecialists, Inc.
54263 Whitaker Boulevard
Jacksonville, FL 32234

Dear Ms. Turner-White:

Eager to pursue a career in environmental engineering, I am interested in the public works inspector training position advertised in the June 19 *Times Herald*.

As a recent graduate of the University of Florida's Environmental Engineering program, I possess the required academic background, and my work experience has given me a solid beginning for pursuing a career in this field. I focused my college coursework to expand my structural and ECS knowledge beyond that required. I also took courses in public planning, geology, geography, and landscape architecture to complete a minor in Environmental Studies. I enhanced my drafting, design, and public relations skills through a summer internship with the U.S. Environmental Protection Agency's engineering division.

I am currently employed part-time as an engineering specialist with the EPA, and am interested in other positions that would expand my knowledge and experience. The enclosed resume outlines additional skills and qualifications that will help me make a strong contribution to EcoSpecialists. I am hardworking and eager to learn, with good communication and people skills. I work well in team situations and require limited supervision.

I would greatly appreciate an opportunity to talk with you and further demonstrate how I can effectively fulfill your organization's needs. I can be reached at the phone number listed above. I look forward to hearing from you. Thank you for your time and consideration.

Sincerely,

Erika Waters

– HARRISON WELLER –

3553 43RD STREET WEST • PORTERFIELD, MICHIGAN 48230
WORK: (616) 555-0988 • HOME: (616) 555-3387
E-MAIL: HWELLER@XXX.COM

February 14, 20__

Ms. Andrea Marks
President
Michigan Environmental Institute
P.O. Box 2247
Detroit, Michigan 48233

Dear Ms. Marks:

I am very interested in working with the Michigan Environmental Institute in your environmental health and safety department. I am submitting this letter in application for the environmental safety specialist position currently being advertised. I specialize in remedial investigations and feasibility studies, ranging from initial assessment to design and implementation.

My background includes experience in formation evaluations, stratigraphic profiling, borehole geophysical surveys, groundwater analysis, and data acquisition and processing.

Environmental knowledge and experience include the following:
- Storage, transportation, and survey of radioactive sources, including attendant record keeping.
- Handling, storage, and transportation of explosives and explosive materials.
- Familiarity with RCRA, CERCLA, SARA, TSCA, NRC, ATF, DOT, and similar regulations and regulating agencies.
- Scientific analysis of borehole geophysical data and the application of interpretation to properly describe hydrogeologic conditions.
- Market development activities, including client studies and market assessments.
- Preparing and presenting presentations to senior management.

Please review my background relative to your requirements and contact me if you would like to talk further. I can be reached at (616) 555-0988 during working hours, and I look forward to hearing from you soon.

Sincerely,

Harrison Weller
Enclosure

Samuel Hacker, P.E.

667 Winston Ave.
St. Louis, MO 63121
(314) 555-3411

April 22, 20__

Marc Ferris
Vice President
S&L Technology Associates, Inc.
Rt. 5, Box 1265
St. Louis, MO 63102

Dear Mr. Ferris:

I am sending you my resume to consider for any suitable openings that S&L Technology Associates may have in the near future.

In addition to my management and technical skills, I have had considerable experience in project development, new business development, and the implementation of new environmental technology. During the past seven years I also have had extensive experience in the solid waste management field, with in-depth involvement in medical, industrial, and municipal waste handling; incineration; energy recovery; and pollution control projects.

I believe my experience in many facets of the environmental field—including project design, procurement, scheduling, and construction—will allow me to make a significant contribution to your operations. Also, my extensive background in electrical and process control systems has given me a well rounded understanding of most chemical, thermal, and physical processes.

I am available for immediate employment and can travel extensively or relocate as required. I look forward to hearing from you and learning more about any current openings for which I am qualified.

Yours sincerely,

Samuel Hacker

Enclosure: Resume

J. William Clark

4437 White Oaks Drive
Urbana, IL 61801
Daytime (217) 555-2847
Evening (217) 555-3345

June 16, 20___

Mr. Arthur Davidson
Director
Organization for Environmental Policy
Suite 110, Ridley Tower
Chicago, Illinois 60621

Dear Mr. Davidson:

I was delighted to talk with you yesterday about your interest in hiring a public affairs director, and I want to restate my interest in learning more about the position.

So that you might learn more about my background, I have enclosed a summary resume for your review. If you prefer, I can forward my complete dossier, along with recommendations from professional associates.

What captures my interest about this position is the possibility for effecting change on a significant scale. My previous experiences have offered tremendous opportunity for influencing the country's growth in positive ways, but within fairly limited spheres—education and domestic economics, primarily—though I have done some work on environmental issues in the past. I am more convinced than ever that there is a great need for an organization such as yours to turn its attention to unifying these issues in a direct and meaningful way. I would find that challenge immensely rewarding, both personally and professionally.

Our mutual friend, Helen Ashwood, told me I could find no more professional and respected an organization with which to align my efforts. After the discussion you and I shared yesterday, I clearly agree with her assessment. Therefore, I look forward to talking with you again soon.

Sincerely,

Bill Clark

Faith Nuygen

775 SW Tilbury Road • Fresno, California 93723
(209) 555-7623 • Nuygen@xxx.com

July 4, 20__

Ms. Ellen Carlson
Senior Director
California Department of Agriculture
One Government Plaza
Sacramento, California 95813

Dear Ms. Carlson:

Thank you for the information you sent in regard to the Project Manager's position with the California Department of Agriculture (CDA). I would like to submit the enclosed application and resume for your further consideration.

I have worked with the Consortium of California Counties since 1993, and I believe I have found my niche in the area of project management. I have handled a wide range of projects with increasing levels of managerial responsibility. Most recently, I directed the planning, coordination, and management of a major statewide conference on environmental regulations, which involved the participation of several international specialists. I was given less than two months to manage the entire project, and yet the result received appreciative reviews from all participants.

After ten very rewarding years with the consortium, however, I am aware that I have reached the extent of opportunities for advancement within the organization. Therefore, I am looking forward to new challenges, and would very much like to join the impressive program at CDA.

I can be reached at (209) 555-2984 during the day, and at the number above for messages as well as evenings and weekends. I look forward to hearing from you and discussing how I might contribute to your program.

Sincerely,

Faith Nuygen

DEBORAH SUMMERS

226 W. Cray Drive
Martinez, California 94552
510-555-2203

September 21, 20__

Ms. Anne Sherman
Executive Director
Jackson Hole Land Trust
P.O. Box 2897
Jackson, Wyoming 83001

Dear Ms. Sherman:

I am writing to inquire about opportunities available in resource management with the Jackson Hole Land Trust. I have read about your organization in various publications, and am impressed with your dedication to protecting open spaces from overgrazing. I would like to be a part of your team very much.

My background in rangeland resource management focused on the restoration, improvement, conservation, ecology, and use of rangelands. Integrated land use, with the essential goal of protecting the land, anchored my educational program. I recently graduated from the University of California, Santa Cruz, which has an exceptional faculty known for taking tough stands to ensure that succeeding generations will benefit from the land.

I would be delighted to travel to Jackson to speak with you about my qualifications. I hope my enthusiasm for this work is apparent. Thank you for your consideration, and I hope to hear from you soon.

Sincerely yours,

Deborah Summers

Tara Westlake
233 S. First Street
Provo, Utah 84602
801-555-2216
twestlake@xxx.com

November 24, 20__

Stan Heron
Wildlife Biologist III
Utah State Department of Wildlife
Region 3
State Resources Building
Salt Lake City, Utah 84122

Dear Mr. Heron:

I spoke with you last summer regarding volunteer work with the Utah State
Department of Wildlife, and you referred me to Len Hughes. I followed up on
that recommendation and enjoyed an extremely informative and beneficial
summer helping with classification projects on the Upper Utah Wildlife
Refuge. Thank you again for the suggestion.

I am writing to you now to explore employment opportunities with the
Department of Wildlife. The enclosed resume will provide you with details
concerning my education, experience, and capabilities.

As you will note, I am seeking a position in wildlife management and research.
I am confident the combination of my training and experience will make me an
asset to the department. I would appreciate the opportunity to meet with you in
person to discuss your needs and organizational objectives, as well as my abilities to fulfill them. I have employment obligations until the middle of April,
and wish to be considered for your next suitable opening at that time.

Thank you for your time and consideration. I look forward to hearing from
you.

Sincerely yours,

Tara Westlake

DAVID HART

2215 Salmon River Road
Olympia, Washington 98110

January 30, 20___

Stephen Miller
Director
Big Sky Bird Observatory
Whitefish, Montana 59938

Dear Mr. Miller:

I am writing to express my interest in obtaining a seasonal position with the Big Sky Bird Observatory. I worked with Susan Jameson this past fall in the Farallon Islands. Her glowing account of the work being done at Big Sky prompted me to write.

I am a wildlife biologist with a background in ornithology and entomology. For the past year and a half, I have been conducting field work for the Point Reyes Bird Observatory, and more recently for the National Audubon Society's Bird Populations Research Project. I have enjoyed working independently and as part of a team, in research both in and out of the field. I have also gladly participated in any educational programs offered at Point Reyes.

Studies such as the Big Sky program interested me greatly, in part for the implications such data may have for biomonitoring research and conservation on a local, national, and global scale.

I hope you will consider me for one of your summer or fall positions, and I look forward to talking with you.

Sincerely,

David Hart
(206) 555-2294

March 12, 20__

Sandra Brown
Recruiting and Staffing
CH 1J26
Wildlife Biologist
Weyerhaeuser Corporation
Tacoma, WA 98477

Dear Ms. Brown:

I received your name from my thesis adviser at Mississippi State University, Jack Myer. He suggested that my educational training and experience would provide the needed background for Weyerhaeuser's Wildlife Biologist position under the Manager of Environmental Forestry.

I recently completed all work toward a master's degree in Wildlife Biology, which will be awarded next month. I also hold a bachelor's degree in Environmental Resource Management from the University of Washington. Upon graduation, I worked for five years as a Forest Ranger, with responsibilities for wildlife management in the Humboldt National Forest in northern California.

I have excellent research skills, both field and laboratory, and have had ample experience with statistical data analysis throughout my graduate degree program. My written communications skills are also strong, and I have successfully taught undergraduate biology classes to college students as well as environmental education seminars to professionals.

As described in the position announcement I received, this opportunity sounds like an ideal fit both for my qualifications and for my professional interests and objectives. I can relocate or travel as needed, and would be delighted to meet with you in Washington to further discuss my qualifications.

Thank you for your consideration. I look forward to talking with you soon.

Sincerely,

Brenna Vincent
434 W. Magnolia Terrace
Jackson, Mississippi 39213
601/555-2293

Thomas Becker

P.O. Box 254
Bozeman, MT 59331
t-becker@xxx.com

May 15, 20__

Eric Miles
Whitefish Point Wildlife Refuge
RR 48, Box 115
Paradise, MI 49768

Dear Mr. Miles:

I am writing to apply for the position of assistant biologist listed in the December edition of the *American Ornithologists' Union Newsletter*. The position that interests me involves the study to document the spring migration at the northeastern tip of the Upper Peninsula of Michigan.

I recently graduated from the University of Wisconsin-Madison with a bachelor's degree in Environmental Biology and have an extensive background in ecology. I spent this past summer at the Flathead Lake Biological Station, where I took an intensive eight-week course entitled Ecology of Birds, taught by Dr. Anne Stuart, a noted international authority on avian ecology and editor of the *International Ornithologist*. My interest in studying birds and their behavior has stretched over 15 years, and the avian ecology aspects of this position intrigue me.

Please find enclosed with this letter a resume that summarizes my qualifications, training, and experiences. I am a well-organized and independent researcher, as well as a quick and enthusiastic learner. I work well under strenuous field conditions and look forward to the challenges of a demanding field position such as this one.

I would like to arrange an interview at your earliest convenience. My telephone number is (406) 555-2203, and I can be reached there any morning before 10:00. Thank you for your consideration, I hope to speak with you soon.

Sincerely,

Thomas Becker

SUSANA MARSTON

14555 Birch Lane
Durham, New Hampshire 03824
Daytime: 603-555-3892, ext. 2899

July 8, 20__

Dr. Richard Knowlton
Professor of Environmental Science
University of New Hampshire
Durham, New Hampshire 03824

Dear Dr. Knowlton:

I am writing to apply for the research associate position announced in the last issue of the alumni magazine. Enclosed please find my resume and three letters of recommendation.

I graduated from UNH in 1990 with a degree in Biology, and have been employed here as a field and research technician, laboratory assistant, and currently as a scientific technician for the Department of Forest Biology. I am very interested in the position in environmental science because it offers expanded challenges in a field that has fascinated me for some time.

I am experienced with a wide range of field, laboratory, and data analysis research techniques, including electron microscopy, darkroom photography, image analysis systems, statistical analyses, and sample collection and identification. These skills exceed the requirements listed in the position announcement, as do my ten years of experience in doing scientific research work.

My extension is 2899 on campus if you would like to call to discuss my qualifications and interest in your work. I look forward to hearing from you and thank you for your consideration.

Sincerely,

Susana Marston

Felice Anthony

3442 South Bridge Road • North Tonawanda, NY 14120 • 716-555-1093

September 19, 20__

Sherry Colwell
Administrative Coordinator
Environmental Action, Inc.
6930 Carroll Avenue, 6th Floor
Tacoma Park, MD 20912

Dear Ms. Colwell:

Please accept the enclosed resume and letters of reference in application for the staff scientist position announced in your latest newsletter. I have long admired the work of your organization, and have decided that I would like to add what talents I have in the areas of science and environmental policy management to these endeavors.

Since 1993 I have worked as a research specialist on a variety of projects, but the work that has most held my interest has involved the isolation of hazardous isotopes found in toxic waste. It has become increasingly clear to me that few in policy-making positions realize how much there is to be concerned about in the disposal and transportation of toxic and hazardous waste.

I would like to further discuss the position and how I might best serve the needs of the organization. I will call early next week to arrange an appointment at your convenience. I look forward to meeting with you and your colleagues.

Thank you for your consideration.

Sincerely,

Felice Anthony

Karel P. Margolise

2893 Puma Street   Davis, CA 95616   (916) 555-3923

November 3, 20__

June Demorest
Fisheries Director
American Rivers
801 Pennsylvania Avenue, SE, Suite 400
Washington, DC 20003

Dear Ms. Demorest:

I am writing to apply for the fisheries biologist position at American Rivers. I am a Native American who has worked extensively with fisheries biology research as well as the issues of resource management, treaty rights, and public policy. I believe this background makes me an ideal candidate for the position described in the Sunday, June 17, edition of the *New York Times*.

As part of the Indian Forest Management Assessment Team, I conducted a congressionally mandated study of the condition and management of Indian forest trust lands. This project involved site visits, personal interviews, and final assessments regarding 15 reservations and native Alaska corporations. As follow-up to the project, I have been working with Native American foresters and conservationists to implement the recommended programs.

American Rivers has demonstrated dedication to a river stewardship ethic, as well as involvement in the preservation of treaty rights. Both positions have influenced me to wish to join your program. I would appreciate receiving your call at the number below, and I look forward to talking with you further about the program and my qualifications.

Thank you for your consideration.

Sincerely,

Karel P. Margolis

CLARA B. DUNNING

186 Montgomery Street
Iowa City, IA 52242
319-555-2341
C.B.Dunning@xxx.com

December 18, 200__

Dr. Kelley Freeman
Eco-Design Consulting, Inc.
2655 S. 18th Street
Chicago, IL 60602

Dear Dr. Freeman:

Please find enclosed a resume and letters of recommendation that I submit to you in application for the environmental scientist position with your consulting firm.

As you will see from the resume, I have more than nine years of experience as a research scientist in the field of environmental science. My bachelor's degree in Environmental Science and Chemistry led me into work with The Institute of Environmental Toxicology. I also have worked with a nonprofit research organization involved in avian research and the impact of pesticides on bird populations.

I understand from one of your colleagues, Walt Fosque, that a great deal of your work involves pesticides and other toxic substances and their impact on the environment. I would bring to your consulting work a specialization in environmental toxicology, although I am experienced in biological science as well.

I am very interested in talking with you and would be happy to travel to Chicago to meet with you in person. Please call or write at the number and address above to arrange a time at your convenience.

Thank you for your consideration.

Yours sincerely,

Clara B. Dunning

#12